T0061012

Blessings

A Devotional Inspired by the Imitation of Christ

ALAN CARRUTH

WestBow Press books may be ordered through booksellers or by contacting:

WestBow Press
A Division of Thomas Nelson & Zondervan
1663 Liberty Drive
Bloomington, IN 47403
www.westbowpress.com
844-714-3454

ISBN: 978-1-6642-7775-5 (sc)
ISBN: 978-1-6642-7776-2 (hc)
ISBN: 978-1-6642-7774-8 (e)

Library of Congress Control Number: 2022916777

Print information available on the last page.

WestBow Press rev. date: 10/06/2022

Contents

Introduction

As I was rereading *The Imitation of Christ* by Thomas à Kempis, I decided—or rather was moved—to start journaling on the various subject matters presented in the devotions. This was a prayerful journey as I asked the Holy Spirit to help me encounter the spiritual truths being presented in a deeper and more meaningful way. As I began journaling, I found the desire to convert the text into more modern and perhaps a little more Protestant language. I began to notice that the process of journaling on these insightful writings began to transform and reorganize my thinking into a simpler and more straightforward understanding of God's wisdom and truth. After finishing my first draft, I started wondering if this wisdom might be helpful to others seeking to become more like Jesus. This decision started a three-year process of revisions as I read and reread *The Imitation of Christ* while allowing the Holy Spirit to inspire and correct my first efforts. I then began searching scripture for appropriate passages that addressed the devotional message being presented. The current book is the result of six revisions in the hopes that God is truly glorified and the reader is enlightened as to what it means to be a disciple of our Lord Jesus. My journey is far from over as I continue to read these words as part of my daily spiritual discipline. I pray that you find challenge, comfort, and peace as you receive assurance in your journey with God.

Blessings,
Alan Carruth

Imitating Christ

When Jesus spoke again to the people, he said, "I am the light of the world. Whoever follows me will never walk in darkness, but will have the light of life."

—JOHN 8:12 (NIV)

As disciples of our Lord Jesus, we, who have formerly indulged in many choices, have chosen to become apprentices to our Master in order to learn the ways of eternal life, but do we really understand what this means? Jesus has called us to come out of the darkness and be bathed in the light of His teaching. For us to understand, we must be freed from the blindness common to us all, allow our minds to be enlightened by the truths of God, and commit to becoming obedient to Jesus's commands. We must seriously choose the way of prayer, scripture study, and fellowship with a faith community if we are to receive understanding concerning the necessity of the Holy Spirit, which brings clarity to God's will. This is the path of divine enlightenment for the disciple who wants to receive understanding concerning the ways of God. Knowing Jesus as the way, truth, and life we so desperately need is critical for recognizing the vain pursuits of humankind. This requires us to pursue the truth of God above all human opinion and advice.

We must also recognize that knowing God's truth is not enough to make us holy—that is, set apart for godly service. We must commit to reflecting the image of Jesus by living devoted to loving and forgiving others. Knowing the whole Bible and all principles of theology is useless unless we show others the grace and love of God. Our lives are doomed to consuming the vanity of humankind unless we become devoted to the ways of Jesus and to the production of good spiritual fruit.

Scripture is full of godly wisdom that reveals our purpose in life, which is to seek the kingdom of God above all other pursuits. We are to live pleasing our Creator, which requires us to take the blinders from our eyes and know well the ways of sin. We must come to recognize the many unprofitable things we chase without God's guidance. For example, it is vanity for us to put our trust in riches that perish or to pursue honor to satisfy our sinful pride. It is vanity to give in to our lusts and allow them to guide us to temporal pleasures that bring severe consequences and regret. It is vanity to live a greedy life hoarding all for self while showing no concern for the needs of others. It is vanity to manipulate others for self-satisfaction and never learn the true meaning of love found only by abiding in God, our source of life and eternal joy. If we claim to be followers of Jesus, shouldn't we allow His counsel to guide us from our vain and sinful ways to heavenly treasures?

Dear disciple, isn't it time for us to become resolute in our loyalty to God, turn our hearts from the vanities of the world, and become imitators of our Lord Jesus? Shouldn't we commit ourselves to learning and practicing our Savior's ways and let our words and deeds bring glory to our God? Isn't it time for us to fully receive the grace of God that soothes our troubled minds and strengthens us against the temptation to satisfy our selfish passions? Let us resolve to abide in our God and know divine love and forgiveness. Let us allow our God to heal our guilty conscience with the Holy Spirit's loving touch and change our sin-stained lives into ones as white as snow.

Humility

Blessed are the meek, For they shall inherit the earth.

—MATTHEW 5:5 (NKJV)

As disciples of our Lord Jesus, we must come to grips with the fact that success in following the path so carefully laid out by our Savior requires the attitude of humility. Practicing humility can prove to be quite challenging since we are so used to seeing our world though proud, arrogant eyes. True understanding comes only with humility, no matter the book or teacher. Unless we allow God to mold and shape our understanding through the lens of humility, we will likely misuse or abuse our knowledge solely to elevate ourselves at the expense of others. Jesus promises us a place of honor when we choose the way of humility, and that honor comes when we learn to be satisfied with anonymous service. Humility is lost on the proud intellectual whose only purpose is to prove their superiority and self-worth. Unless we allow God to divinely guide us into humble service, our focus will be on self-glory as we seek the praise of others rather than seeking to serve as the least of these.

Humility brings divine truth to our thinking as we hear God proclaim that having all worldly knowledge without charity toward others profits nothing for God's kingdom. Proud knowledge inspires life's delusions that bring a troubled mind full of worry and fear. Gaining humble eyes allows us to have compassion even for those who we would otherwise deem unlovable. We understand that knowledge is essential for a successful life, but without God, we exchange a joyful, satisfying life full of meaning and purpose for a life of poor choices, regret, and despair. When we pursue a humble life inspired by God, we discover the rich rewards of peace of mind and a clear conscience. By allowing our minds to be ruled by humility, we are empowered to get over ourselves and give up our proud and arrogant ways. Our lives become filled with thanks and praise to our awesome God, who is the source of all our gifts and talents. When we allow godly wisdom to enlighten our minds, we truly understand the limits of our understanding. This revelation should bring us to our knees, and in humility, we should admit that we are ignorant about so many things.

Dear disciple, blessed humility is actually a position of power, for it allows God to fill us with the Holy Spirit. We should, therefore, adopt a humble attitude in order to receive God's counsel and comprehend divine wisdom and revelation. Let us allow God to help us see outside ourselves so that we release the ugliness found in our superior judgment of others. Let us hear Jesus tell us that passing judgment on others is sinful and wrong, for we are no less guilty of the same acts. In humility, let us admit that we are sinners and that we are saved from our hopeless condition only by the redeeming gift of Jesus, who came not to be served but to serve and to give His life as a ransom for you and for me.

Truth

Teach me your way, Lord, that I may rely on your faithfulness; give me an undivided heart, that I may fear your name. I will praise you, Lord my God, with all my heart; I will glorify your name forever. For great is your love toward me; you have delivered me from the depths, from the realm of the dead.

—PSALM 86:11–13 (NIV)

As disciples of our Lord Jesus, we believe that ultimate truth comes to us from God through scripture and the glory of creation, so why do we place such value in the opinions and speculations of the so-called experts of the world, be they Christian or secular? Does any good come from arguing over opinions and speculations concerning the uncertainties of life at the expense of the kingdom of God? Why are we so consumed with petty and irrelevant things? These discussions are not focused on the godly ways of joy or peace but on our disgust or disappointment concerning a wide range of issues. The result of these useless exchanges is discontent, anxiety, and worry. Unless we allow the Holy Spirit to refocus our conversations on godly truths, we risk straining our relationships to the point of breaking for the sake of our prideful, arrogant opinions. By failing to restrain our divisive thinking, we allow corrupt reasoning to cloud our views of humanity in general and individuals in particular. Our capacity to love and forgive for the sake of God's kingdom is lost to us as we cast judgment upon those who refuse to agree with our truth.

We are charged with seeking God's truth in scripture so that we can be set free from our faulty thinking. Much in scripture is difficult to understand or is easily misinterpreted, which requires us to seek help from a community of faith so that we are guided into proper understanding as to the ways of life, worship, and praise of our God. We must understand that we are incapable of comprehending the way of Jesus unless we allow our minds to be renewed by the Holy Spirit. This path frees our minds and enables us to see and hear God's Word and creation speak lessons of life to us. Without God's divine wisdom, our judgment concerning kingdom living is questionable at best, but when we allow scripture to become our primary source of truth concerning all things, we see that the ways of Jesus are the path to a joy-filled life. We must learn that the peace of mind we so desperately desire is found only in the assurance of God's truth acquired by the abiding presence of our God.

Dear disciple, let us confess that life-giving truth is found in God alone. Let us earnestly pursue the path of becoming one with God so that divine truth becomes our reality. Let us accept Jesus's invitation to receive the Holy Spirit and abide in God's presence, where we experience God's everlasting love. Let us become obedient to the ways of Jesus and revel in the Holy Spirit's guidance. Let us exchange our unworthy opinions for the truth of God and be empowered to deal with the many worrisome and exasperating situations of life. Let us pray for the Holy Spirit to come and fill us so that we might hear the psalmist's words of abiding truth. "Be still and know that I am God" (Psalm 46:10 NKJV).

Simple Faith

Then people brought little children to Jesus for him to place his hands on them and pray for them. But the disciples rebuked them. Jesus said, "Let the little children come to me, and do not hinder them, for the kingdom of heaven belongs to such as these."

—MATTHEW 19:13–14 (NIV)

As disciples of our Lord Jesus, it is critical for us to look in the mirror and see if our relationship with God is becoming more childlike. We might consider this a useless endeavor unless we admit that our minds have become cluttered with busyness that hinders our receiving the true, life-giving wisdom of God. Jesus would have us return to a state of carefree wonder concerning the world so that we might more easily receive guidance on the truly important things of life. Childlike trust allows God to change how we see ourselves and, more importantly, how we see others by moving us away from our self-centered world. Childlike faith in God redirects our motives toward accomplishing those things pleasing to God rather than pleasing only ourselves. This change of heart allows God to show us our bias and prejudice and starts the process of healing our often troubled and anxious minds.

The more we devote our life to God, the more we understand that, like a child, we need help with every aspect of life. We must let God enlighten our distorted, reasoning minds so that we see the impossibility of mastering our sinful inclinations without help. We must develop a daily routine of seeking God's help for guidance and strength in order to succeed in the overcoming life for which we were created. Even as we make progress toward the goal of becoming like Jesus, we must never forget that darkness is always lurking. We will encounter many so-called "truths" in our quest for the overcoming life, but the disciple with childlike faith sees God's truth as a guide to a life of love, forgiveness, compassion, and generosity. God has ordained for us to live in harmony as a community that reflects the ways of Jesus; therefore, we must dedicate ourselves to understanding what it means to live a virtuous life—a life that is pleasing to God.

Dear disciple, let us never forget to prayerfully invite God into our study and ask over and over again for help in understanding the virtuous life. Let us ask the Holy Spirit to enable us in reclaiming our childlike faith so that God might reshape our understanding. Let us ask Jesus to give us the attitude of humility so that our faith would be simple and unassuming, empowering us to be more faithful and obedient in love. Let us examine our big words and complex theologies and ask if we are using them to build the kingdom of God or to simply show everyone our arrogant superiority.

Our Passion

Those who belong to Christ Jesus have crucified the flesh with its passions and desires. Since we live by the Spirit, let us keep in step with the Spirit. Let us not become conceited, provoking and envying each other.

—GALATIANS 5:24–26 (NIV)

As disciples of our Lord Jesus, do we seriously examine our passions on a regular basis? Does our daily routine reflect a concern for changing our priorities? Do we continue to consume worldly entertainment at the expense of knowing God's Word? Do we indulge in gossip and divisive arguments over petty matters instead of sharing the ways of Jesus? Do we still allow our lustful passions control over our decisions instead of nailing them to the cross? What would happen if we allowed our passions to shift from satisfying our sinful desires to fulfilling God's desires? Are we just lazy, or do we just not understand the requirements for becoming more like Jesus? As a child of God, shouldn't we be greatly concerned with how we reflect ourselves to others? On the Day of Judgment, do we really expect God to be impressed by all of our selfish accomplishments? We know full well that God will be looking for a life full of love, forgiveness, compassion, and generosity, so shouldn't we value the things God values? Shouldn't we repent of our sinful ways and devote ourselves to humble service in building God's kingdom?

The time has come for us to give up our lame excuses and appreciate the difficulty in overcoming our selfish passions. If we are going to claim disciple status for ourselves, we must pour our time and energy into prayer, scripture study, and especially sharing life's difficulties with fellow disciples. Time is fleeting, so our value system must change quickly. Honestly, how long will our worldly insights and accomplishments be remembered? Shouldn't we appreciate how quickly the glory of the world passes away? Shouldn't we be concerned with doing God's will and becoming passionate in glorifying God's kingdom instead of pursuing vain, worldly pleasures or achieving self-glory?

Dear disciple, to be great in God's eyes is to be one who has great charity. Let us become passionate about righteousness and holiness and allow the Holy Spirit to enlighten us concerning our loyalties. Let us welcome the valued high honor of being counted as the least of these. Let us become truly wise and devote our lives to reflecting Jesus to the world and reject a life that consumes all the world offers. Let us let our passions be directed toward abiding in our God and renounce our sinful ways. The ways of God are the only ways to satisfy our desire for joy and peace of mind.

WISDOM

My goal is that they may be encouraged in heart and united in love, so that they may have the full riches of complete understanding, in order that they may know the mystery of God, namely, Christ, in whom are hidden all the treasures of wisdom and knowledge. I tell you this so that no one may deceive you by fine-sounding arguments.

—COLOSSIANS 2:2–4 (NIV)

Wisdom can be defined as knowledge and experience that lead to good judgment and sound decision-making with regard to our actions. As disciples of our Lord Jesus, we might speak of wisdom as the application of God's divine revelation in guiding our actions to nurture His kingdom. Unfortunately, we face the difficult task of overcoming our vast secular knowledge and experience, which often clashes with Jesus's teachings. Scripture warns us to be shrewd in our understanding of the self-centered ways of humankind so that we are on guard against any evil motives and respond to life's situations in a godly manner. It is a sad thing to see people being lured into unpleasantness by those gifted with authoritative and eloquent speech.

As disciples, we are charged with knowing and doing God's will rather than pursuing human delusions that tickle our fancy and incite harsh and evil deeds toward others. Once we have been captivated by the truth of God, we should not allow ourselves to indulge in the ways of the world any longer. We should recognize our human weakness and learn to trust in the power of God's truth to set us free from this horrid behavior. The strength for godly action comes only by dwelling in the presence of God in prayer and daily scripture reading and by bonding with those faithful to Jesus. Only then will we be free from obstinate opinions, rash actions, and vicious gossip.

Dear disciple, let us stop relying on our own cleverness and take counsel from God's Word. Let us earnestly seek advice from the wise and godly members of our faith community and stop following our own inclinations. Let us give up our prideful, selfish ways and turn to our blessed Lord Jesus's teachings for guidance into life. This is the path that empowers us with humility and blessed wisdom for God's glory. Our example might even be the inspiration for others to seek the peace and harmony found in the kingdom of God here on earth. Let us be willing to surrender our self-righteous egos and allow ourselves to be captivated by our God. Let us become fully equipped with the armor of God so that our joy becomes complete as worthy servants of our Master.

Reading God's Word

All Scripture is God-breathed and is useful for teaching, rebuking, correcting and training in righteousness, so that the servant of God may be thoroughly equipped for every good work.

—2 TIMOTHY 3:16–17 (NIV)

As disciples of our Lord Jesus, we are instructed to receive godly wisdom through daily scripture reading, for this is how we discover the truth about ourselves, the truth about our God, and the truth concerning our relationships. In reading scripture, we must have an eager and receptive mind so that God's revelation can transform our thinking into life changing truth. We rob ourselves of God's blessings if our only goal in reading scripture is simply to obtain factual knowledge. A mind that resists the urging of the Holy Spirit through scripture remains blind to the needs of others and is often guilty of using God's Word to assault and belittle others for their "inferior" understanding. As we read scripture, it is beneficial to ask the Holy Spirit to help us understand the intended message, for time, culture, and human interpretations can be obstacles to God's revelations. It is also helpful to read other inspired writings to help us understand, for we never know when or where profound godly truth will find us.

It is important for us to remember that patience is required on our part in reading scripture, for full understanding is often hidden from us for a time. The Bible is a diverse collection of inspired writings from numerous authors and is written in many different styles spanning thousands of years. Seeming contradictions often appear in scripture, which can result in frustration and confusion. It is often better to pass over what we do not understand for a time and focus on what God clearly expects from us. If we allow God to enlighten our minds, our thinking will eventually be transformed enough to receive the Holy Spirit's revelation.

Dear disciple, let us understand that the most profitable way to receive truth from scripture is to read with humility, simplicity, and faith. Let us resolve to be changed by scripture reading rather than to become puffed up by our "superior" understanding, for this can lead to the misuse of God's Word against others. Let us admit our need for godly wisdom to correct our sinful behavior. Let us seek willingly and listen attentively to the words of the saints of old so carefully preserved for us. Let us wholeheartedly accept Jesus's call to "follow me" and learn the path found in scripture. Let us live into the blessed state of knowing the way, the truth, and the life of Jesus and receive the blessings of relationship found in God and neighbor.

Desiring God First

Hear, O Israel: The Lord is our God, the Lord alone. You shall love the Lord your God with all your heart, and with all your soul, and with all your might. Keep these words that I am commanding you today in your heart. Recite them to your children and talk about them when you are at home and when you are away, when you lie down and when you rise. Bind them as a sign on your hand, fix them as an emblem on your forehead, and write them on the doorposts of your house and on your gates.

—DEUTERONOMY 6:4–9 (NRSV)

As disciples of our Lord Jesus, do we, by our actions, demonstrate that we love our God with our whole being? Have we rightly considered the benefits to loving God above all else? We may say that we believe that God created us for a purpose, but we often struggle in finding satisfaction while performing our many duties in life. By loving our God first and foremost, we open ourselves to receiving vital instruction concerning what it means to love others, which is something very dear to our Creator. This fact should give us a clue as to our purpose in life. Scripture clearly states that when we place our desires first and foremost in our God and commit to obeying the ways of Jesus, we will be blessed with divine insight concerning loving others. Having the guiding presence of God in our lives is critical to understanding our purpose in the kingdom of heaven. It is unfortunate that secular society, for the most part, encourages us to choose for ourselves the path of life with the slogan "Whatever makes you happy." God created us with desires and the freedom to choose how we reach satisfaction, but if we are not taught and shown that loving God with our whole being is the only way to truly find the joy of living, we will choose our way, which usually leads us to lusting after and coveting the created things of God rather than advancing the kingdom of God through love.

Here in lies our problem in finding a satisfactory purpose in life. We are told to pursue the things that make us happy and then are given a smorgasbord of things from which to choose. Many of these things are not, in and of themselves, bad, but without God, they fail to satisfy the deep longing only God can fill. Our love of God is the guiding truth to satisfaction of purpose in all the decisions we make. Unless we allow God to guide our thinking, our selfishness will lead us into lustful, covetous choices that ultimately cause worry, anxiety, and remorse over our failures to live up to the standards laid out so clearly by Jesus. Hope for our wretched state comes when we finally see Jesus as the Savior who can deliver us from our selfish ways.

Dear disciple, let us understand that our purpose in life is not tied to our job, family, or friends but to loving God and loving as God loves. Without God, our sensual desires drive us far off the path for which we were created, and our relationships suffer for it. Let us stop fooling ourselves by thinking we can find peace of mind and satisfaction of purpose without loving our God above all else. Like the prodigal son, let us come to our senses, hear the wisdom of our Lord Jesus, nail our selfish desires to the cross, and embrace our God. Only by abiding in God's presence will we be freed to pursue our true purpose and find the peace that passes all understanding.

God or False Hope

This is what the Lord Almighty says: "Do not listen to what the prophets are prophesying to you; they fill you with false hopes. They speak visions from their own minds, not from the mouth of the Lord. They keep saying to those who despise me, 'The Lord says: You will have peace.' And to all who follow the stubbornness of their hearts they say, 'No harm will come to you.'"

—JEREMIAH 23:16–17 (NIV)

As disciples of our Lord Jesus, we, of all people, should have a hopeful outlook on life as long as we continue seeking the way of our Savior. By abiding in our God, hope becomes an unwavering assurance in the power of the Holy Spirit that gives us strength to persevere through the many challenges we encounter along life's path. Unfortunately, our prideful minds often convince us to trust in our own wisdom or to seek solutions in self-help resources or from those who know nothing of God. As followers of Jesus, we should quickly learn that hope is not found in the security of wealth, status, or possessions. These things are just a mirage and a stumbling block of false hope. These things, valued by so many, blind us to the truly valuable things God freely offers us. Scripture tells us that our hope is found in the covenant love relationship with our God and our faith community, which we know and experience as the body of

Christ. Once we enter these hope-filled relationships, we see that there is no advantage to high position in life, nor is there shame in the lowest position. We understand that God's assurances come from serving our Lord Jesus in His kingdom. As we participate in service to, fellowship with, and worship of our God, we come to know how weak and needy we are. This revelation should move us to rely completely on God as our hope and our strength. We must constantly receive divine wisdom from the Holy Spirit so that our words and actions more consistently reflect Jesus. Our hope is found in Jesus and His righteousness and not in the advice of scheming individuals full of empty promises.

It takes a humble spirit to turn from the false security found in temporal things and trust in the provisions of God. The promises of eternity are not found in wealth, powerful friends, our stature or physical beauty, our talents, or our athletic skills. These wonderful gifts from God fade with time and fail with illness or injury. Our hope is found in the abiding presence of God alone and in Jesus's promises of salvation and eternal life.

Dear disciple, we are fools if we put our hope and security in the ways of the world. Let us understand that there is no redemption or rescue for us as long as we put our trust in our own wisdom and material possessions. Let us learn the path of humility, for this is the only way toward unfaltering hope. Let us receive the graceful gifts of our God and stop indulging in the false promises of the world. Let us, in humility, commit to the hope-filled life found in following the ways of Jesus so that we can rest assured in the promises of our God.

Friend of the World or of God

You adulterous people, don't you know that friendship with the world means enmity against God? Therefore, anyone who chooses to be a friend of the world becomes an enemy of God.

—JAMES 4:4 (NIV)

You are My friends if you do whatever I command you.

—JOHN 15:14 (NKJV)

As disciples of our Lord Jesus, we should guard ourselves against worldly values that would guide us into unethical or amoral behavior, for therein lies disaster. We become friends of God by intimate prayer, study, and fellowship, which give us discernment concerning the consequences of following the examples of those who have no fear of God. We are so easily tempted to admire the wealthy or dream of mingling with the famous, but the one who has drawn near to God knows that intimacy with the worldly leads to indulging in lust, envy, and suffering. God's holiness standard calls us to be set apart for God's good pleasure, which requires our obedience, but in time, our obedience becomes our good pleasure as well.

Knowing the will of God is essential for our training in discerning the unpleasing and unhelpful things of life. Scripture is clear concerning our need for a faith community's guidance, for other disciples can help lead us through scripture and prayer into a richer knowing of God's presence. We must let go of our old ways and rely on the Holy Spirit to give us eyes to recognize those who would entice us to indulge our sinful desires; otherwise, we remain trapped in our sin. Our sinful condition has no cure other than the presence of God, for without God's divine wisdom and revelation, we are forever vulnerable to the temptations of the world. We must take the apostle Peter's advice to heart and truly believe that our enemy never rests but prowls like a lion ready to devour us!

We must be very discerning as to whom we open our hearts. The best spiritual practice is to find a devout follower of Jesus to act as our guide—someone who is wise and who fears God. God has purposely called us into communities of faith, for therein lies our lifeline. Where else can we turn in confidence to find the ways of the kingdom of God? If we truly desire to become friends of God, we must fully commit ourselves to a life of prayer, scripture reading, and faith community sharing. What joy we receive when we are empowered to overcome the attraction of created things in order to become useful in God's kingdom.

Dear disciple, let us make up our minds to seek our God with all our hearts, souls, minds, and strength. Let us draw near to the humble, devout, and virtuous people of God and pursue edifying things that lead to a life that reflects Jesus to the world. Let us realize that our good character is either built up or corrupted by those with whom we associate. Why should we care if we have a good reputation among scoundrels? Let us get over ourselves and become friends of God so that we might receive Holy Spirit power and enjoy humble kingdom service for the glory of our God.

Obedience and Submission

Know therefore that the Lord your God is God; he is the faithful God, keeping his covenant of love to a thousand generations of those who love him and keep his commandments.

—DEUTERONOMY 7:9 (NIV)

As disciples of our Lord Jesus, have we committed to memory the many commandments ordained by God necessary for our instruction as to living in harmony with others? We are called to daily obedience concerning these required instructions, but there is something about the human condition that often causes us to rebel against authoritative commands. It would appear that our willingness to obey our teachers depends, in part, on how we view them. We see some of our instructors as unsympathetic taskmasters, while others are loving and patient mentors. Our willingness to obey and submit also depends on whether we see the instruction as useful or necessary. If we deem the instruction valuable, we are willing to submit to rigorous, painful training in order to reach our desired goal.

As followers of Jesus, we should know that scripture clearly lays out the benefits of being obedient to God's instructions and the consequences of choosing our own way. Why is it that so many who profess to believe in God show little, if any, evidence of obedience to

God's holy commandments? Those whose lives reflect the ways of Jesus will attest that it is a very great task to give up selfish ways in order to bring glory and honor to God. It would appear that we are guilty of following our own way as long as our needs and wants are satisfied, but as soon as our blindness is revealed and our security is shattered by the consequences of our actions, we are forced to reconsider the truth in our choices.

Once we commit to acting on the teachings of scripture and allow God to prove to us the validity of divine truth, we will truly see that we are sinners in desperate need of a Savior. This is the only way forward for the disciples of Jesus. Blessed obedience and humble submission to Jesus's commands to love and forgive will forever change our lives, allowing divine revelation to flow into us as living water. Scripture will come alive as we see the hand of God move through time. Our so-called truths, which only brought us discontent, grumbling, and complaining, will be replaced with God's eternal truths, which allow us to proclaim that wisdom and strength come from God alone.

Dear disciple, let us no longer be drawn to the company of the selfish whose talk of "greener pastures" only leads to discontentment and a troubled conscience. Let us resolve to seek the counsel of godly men and women who will guide us to the truth found in the ways of Jesus our Lord. Let us pray and meditate before our Father in heaven for strength to give up our pride and obstinance and accept the wise ways of humble obedience. Let us stop giving our God lip service and allow ourselves to become new creations. Let us give up our high opinions of ourselves and allow the Holy Spirit to transform us into the best possible versions of ourselves for God's glory.

Idle Talk

Be diligent to present yourself approved to God, a worker who does not need to be ashamed, rightly dividing the word of truth. But shun profane and idle babblings, for they will increase to more ungodliness.

—2 TIMOTHY 2:15–16 (NKJV)

But no man can tame the tongue. It is an unruly evil, full of deadly poison.

—JAMES 3:8 (NKJV)

As disciples of our Lord Jesus, we are warned to avoid idle talk because of the damage our cavalier speech can cause, but it seems that we take little heed of this warning. We gather and share the latest news to keep everyone informed concerning the things we value, but unless someone sets the boundaries on the subject matters, we often find ourselves on shaky ground by using questionable language or by discussing things that only lead to complaining, bitterness, and divisiveness. Before we speak, we should ask if our words are for building up or tearing down. Gossip means different things to different people, but it is clear that gossip quickly ensnares and captivates us. This should warn us that our human condition would have us remain prideful and arrogant, holding our superior opinions above all others'. Thankfully, once we invite the presence of the Holy Spirit as guide and moderator of our conversations, our conscience is quickly convicted of guilt, which should cause us to seek God's forgiveness in repentance.

As followers of Jesus, we should understand how easily we are drawn into destructive conversations and should, therefore, take the necessary steps to guard our tongues. How often have we wished we had kept our mouth shut! We often seek comfort from our friends to ease our wearied and troubled minds, but if we are not careful, our conversations can take on a hateful tone, which never brings us the peace of mind for which we long. The only solution to our fiery tongues is to have the mind of the risen Christ. We must allow our minds to be flooded with the presence of God if we ever hope to contain our human impulses to speak our unfettered minds and lay waste to our relationships with family, friends, and even our faith communities.

Dear disciple, let us hear the wisdom of scripture and understand how desperately we need help controlling our tongue. Let us truly devote ourselves to following the ways of Jesus and pray that our goal in our time spent together is for love and healing. Let us allow God to put a holy muzzle on our mouths concerning unprofitable things and ask for Holy Spirit guidance so that our words are more than mere wind. As disciples, let us band together in this holy quest and hold each other accountable so that sacred boundaries become easily identified concerning appropriate kingdom speech.

Obtaining the Peace of God

Do not be anxious about anything, but in every situation, by prayer and petition, with thanksgiving, present your requests to God. And the peace of God, which transcends all understanding, will guard your hearts and your minds in Christ Jesus.

—PHILIPPIANS 4:6–7 (NIV)

As disciples of our Lord Jesus, we read in scripture that our Savior desires that we receive a most marvelous gift, the peace of God. At first, we may not appreciate what is being offered until we hear Jesus tell us that our lives should be free of worry, anxiety, and fear. If we examine our often tumultuous lives, we may wonder how this is possible. We must hear Jesus tell us that the root of our problem is our desire-driven choices. It is amazing how blind we can be to the cause of our turmoil and wonder how we arrived at our current situation. In times like these, we long for peace of mind, but in order to receive God's promised peace, we must be honest with ourselves and admit that our covetous choices are to blame for our sorry state.

Jesus tells us that our focus should be on eternal things that build the kingdom of God, yet we continue to be occupied with our own selfish interests. When we refuse to admit that we are full of lust and envy, we have no hope of overcoming the cause of our dilemma. We should be at the foot of the cross with our hearts open wide and receive the truth of our sinful nature, to confess our wrongdoing and lack of trust, and to receive God's forgiveness and strength to overcome. Only in trusting God do we receive divine comforting peace, which leads to a joy filled life.

As followers of Jesus, we should know that there is no divine strength or guidance in empty religious practices and lip service in order to impress others. We need to take an axe to the root of our sin, and that axe is God the Father, our Lord Jesus the Christ, and the Holy Spirit. The gracious gifts of our God are our only hope in overcoming our deluded and stubborn will!

Dear disciple, spiritual progress toward a godly life comes only at the foot of the cross. Let us commit to our transformation by visiting it daily in prayer and meditation. Let us read scripture daily, knowing that God's Word is crucial for divine wisdom and guidance. Let us repent of our waywardness and receive God's forgiveness, love, and revealed truth. Let us embrace the Holy Spirit and be empowered for the overcoming life. Let us grow in our spiritual practices so that our trust in God becomes our new reality. It is by trusting in the assurances of God that we receive peace of mind and the ability to live the life for which we were created.

The Value of Adversity

Remember how the Lord your God led you all the way in the wilderness these forty years, to humble and test you in order to know what was in your heart, whether or not you would keep his commands. He humbled you, causing you to hunger and then feeding you with manna, which neither you nor your ancestors had known, to teach you that man does not live on bread alone but on every word that comes from the mouth of the Lord. Your clothes did not wear out and your feet did not swell during these forty years. Know then in your heart that as a man disciplines his son, so the Lord your God disciplines you.

—DEUTERONOMY 8:2–5 (NIV)

"I have told you these things, so that in me you may have peace. In this world you will have trouble. But take heart! I have overcome the world."

—JOHN 16:33 (NIV)

As we read scripture, it may be surprising to find how often the divinely inspired authors speak of the value of adversity. At first reading, this seems strange; after all, who enjoys going through trials and tribulations? In fact, our usual response to adversity is moaning and complaining and asking, "Why me?" As long as we remain in our stiff-necked ways, we cannot see the benefit of going through adversity. Unless we wake up and turn to God, we will never understand the importance of humility. These troubling times are often sent to remind us that our temporal lives are not to be guided by whims and fancies. We are not to place our hope in worldly things but in things eternal.

As disciples of our Lord Jesus, we must understand that it is for our benefit to suffer, to be mistreated or misjudged, and to be denied credit for our "good works." Our loving and merciful God would have us understand that consolation does not come from things external but from the abiding presence of God alone. Suffering is designed to help us become humble and seek our Savior God, who knows what is necessary for our discipleship. When affliction, temptation, and tormenting evil thoughts come, it is the humble disciple who clearly realizes that their greatest need is guidance and assurance, which is met only by God Almighty and our faith community.

Dear disciple, even though we are saddened by misery and wearied of living, we must never give up hope. We must turn to our God and faith community and give ourselves completely to the abiding presence of the Holy Spirit. We must let go of the idea that security and peace can be found in earthly things and be willing to cry out for mercy, knowing that we are loved and valued by our Creator. Let us humbly know that Holy Spirit power gives us ample strength for patience and perseverance to grow in our times of woe as long as we abide in the presence of our Holy God and enter the perfect rest offered by our Savior.

Temptation

When tempted, no one should say, "God is tempting me." For God cannot be tempted by evil, nor does he tempt anyone; but each person is tempted when they are dragged away by their own evil desire and enticed. Then, after desire has conceived, it gives birth to sin; and sin, when it is full-grown, gives birth to death.

—JAMES 1:13–15 (NIV)

As we study God's Word, right away we witness the plague of humankind in the Garden of Eden: temptation. A serpent—Satan, the devil, call it what you will—whispers reasonable lies to us. "If you pursue this path, your desires will be satisfied." No one is so perfect or holy that they can escape this whispering voice for as long as they dwell on earth. As disciples of our Lord Jesus, we should know that the enemy is more easily conquered when recognized at the threshold and refused admittance to our minds. It is when we allow our minds to dwell on our temptations that the enemy gains strength. At first, temptation begins as a mere thought, but if given reign, it cascades to imagination, pleasure, unbridled desire, and finally consent. Our rescue from our plight is to stop trying to fix ourselves, turn to our Creator, and experience God's healing presence, which purifies our thinking and instructs us in the humble way of life. Scripture tells of the saints of old who testify to the healing power found in God's abiding presence as opposed to those who shun God to indulge in the fleshy desires fanned by their temptations, resulting in a sad life full of pain and regret.

As followers of Jesus, we should know better than to try to just avoid or escape our temptations. Where can we possibly flee, for isn't temptation found everywhere? Even knowing our weakness and making resolutions to overcome temptation is a futile exercise and can leave us feeling even more entrapped in our sin. In our human condition, we are helpless in overcoming temptation with good intentions. Our only hope for our wavering minds is putting our trust in God and praying for mercy and rescue from the enemy. In our own strength, we are nothing and failure is our fate.

Dear disciple, let us admit how vulnerable we are to the enticing, silky-sweet words of temptation that caress our minds toward deplorable acts. Without God's wisdom, our minds are rudderless ships tossed to and fro, leaving us defenseless before our lustful desires. We must put our trust in the presence of the Holy Spirit to strengthen and guide our every thought. Let us resolve to abide continually in God's presence and allow Holy Spirit power to be the anchor that holds us firm in our troubled waters.

Inappropriate Judgment

Do not judge, or you too will be judged. For in the same way you judge others, you will be judged, and with the measure you use, it will be measured to you.

—MATTHEW 7:1–2 (NIV)

As disciples of our Lord Jesus, we are warned of the consequences of judging others, but the fact remains that we are all guilty of this rash behavior. Why do we not listen to Jesus and repent of this hurtful practice? Do we not hear scripture tell us that we are not qualified to judge others? Judgment is reserved for God alone! In our blindness, have we decided that the behavior of others should conform to our unenlightened understanding of correct behavior? As long as we cherish the log in our eye, we will remain blind to the ways of God. How can we expect to reflect Jesus to the world when we refuse to understand what it means to love and forgive? Unless we allow God to enlighten our minds as to the ways of Jesus, our perspective will forever remain clouded with arrogance and selfishness. Instead of judging others, we should be judging ourselves as to whether we are obedient to the godly standard revealed by the life of our Lord and Savior.

If we are to succeed in changing our focus from judging to loving, we must allow the Holy Spirit to possess our minds and reveal the truth of our purpose in life. Our minds must be full of the

Word of God found in scripture so that the Holy Spirit can speak truth to us in our encounters with others. Unless we are devoted to this path, our unbridled emotions will continue to rage when we encounter any opposing opinion leading to much regrettable language. The world is full of objectionable behavior, but if we are to ever find peace of mind, we must relinquish this practice that is reserved for God alone. We cry out to God for justice because of the widespread inhumanity in the world, but when we consider our day-to-day interactions with family, friends, and neighbors, we need God's help to calm our spirits before we discuss our differing views. What a sad state of affairs it is when differences of opinion destroy relationships. As the body of Christ, are we not called to be united in mind and purpose?

Dear disciple, let us remember that God's judgment falls on us as we judge others! Let us humbly submit to the way of Jesus Christ and pray for divine enlightenment so that godly wisdom becomes our guide in communication. Let us stop using our own opinions as judgment standards and admit that we need help in breaking this offensive habit. Blindness to the sin of rash judgment leads to broken relationships and alienation from others. Let us cultivate a life that is pleasing to God. Let us abide in God's faithful love, study scripture, and be transformed by the renewing of our minds so that our words reflect love, forgiveness, and understanding. Let us rise above our human wisdom so that others might see the light of Jesus and give glory to God.

Motivated by Charity

Be careful not to practice your righteousness in front of others to be seen by them. If you do, you will have no reward from your Father in heaven. "So when you give to the needy, do not announce it with trumpets, as the hypocrites do in the synagogues and on the streets, to be honored by others. Truly I tell you, they have received their reward in full. But when you give to the needy, do not let your left hand know what your right hand is doing, so that your giving may be in secret. Then your Father, who sees what is done in secret, will reward you.

—MATTHEW 6:1–4 (NIV)

As disciples of our Lord Jesus, we are instructed to pay careful attention concerning our attitude in showing charity toward the needs of others. Our problem in understanding the seriousness of this subject arises from our lack of God's perspective on the matter of charity. The meaning of charity has changed over the years and is now associated with giving to the needy, but originally it was used to translate the Greek word *agape*. By understanding Jesus's teachings, we should willingly adopt an attitude of giving that reveals God's compassion and love freely given to all. Giving to those in need is always admirable, but the act loses its luster in the eyes of God without charity. Even the smallest gesture of charity is valued by

God, who is pleased by the love that motivates us rather than the deed itself.

If we claim to be followers of Jesus, we should be motivated to love as God loves and be driven by the vision of building the kingdom of God in the here and now. Unfortunately, many good deeds originate from a desire to promote a good appearance, to earn merit, or to receive awards or rewards. As disciples, we must guard against these motives and seek nothing for ourselves but do all for the glory of God. Also, we must not envy the truly charitable for we will be tempted to say unkind and unjustified words about those who do not rejoice in themselves but desire only to glorify God.

Dear disciple, being truly charitable is a precious gift found only by those who devoutly seek God to understand the ways of agape love. Let us strive to know scripture well and remember that all good things flow from God. Let us abide in God the Father and our Lord Jesus and pray, "Come, Holy Spirit" so that we might become a stream of living water ever ready to meet the needs of those so desperately thirsty.

The Burden of Faults

As a prisoner for the Lord, then, I urge you to live a life worthy of the calling you have received. Be completely humble and gentle; be patient, bearing with one another in love. Make every effort to keep the unity of the Spirit through the bond of peace. There is one body and one Spirit, just as you were called to one hope when you were called; one Lord, one faith, one baptism; one God and Father of all, who is over all and through all and in all.

—EPHESIANS 4:1–6 (NIV)

As disciples of our Lord Jesus, we are cautioned concerning fault finding where we feel it necessary to note the imperfections in the reasoning power of others. We must admit that we are good at seeing the faults in others while turning blind eyes to our own imperfections. If left unchecked, faultfinding becomes a self-destructive force that wreaks havoc on those around us. Even as we are made aware of this undesirable imperfection, we find it very difficult to overcome its practice. Faultfinding stems from our human condition for we are a prideful bunch bent on proving our superior understanding in matters both secular and sacred. It is a mystery as to whether this human condition is ordained for us by God, but perhaps it is appointed to test our patience and ability to bear the burden of others' faults. We cannot know all that God has in store for us to help us mature in the Christian walk, but we must have faith and trust in the ways of our Creator.

One thing is clear to those who choose to receive God's wisdom on this matter. We are commanded to bear patiently with the faults and weaknesses of others, whatever they may be. After all, we too have many defects that others must endure. We must admit our weakness in overcoming our pettiness and seek God's help in changing the way we think and act toward others. It is so amazing that, in our arrogance, we think we can bend others to our will by constantly pointing out their shortcomings. Why do we expect others to be perfect while failing to correct our own faults? We are anxious for others to endure severe correction but refuse to look in the mirror ourselves. We take great offense at others' freedom to offend but do not deny ourselves the same liberty! We would bind them with rules and laws but allow ourselves to be unrestrained in all we say and do. What hypocrites we are!

Dear disciple, scripture clearly states that we will suffer critical and unkind words but that we are not to respond in kind. We are called to bear patiently with each other's faults and offer corrective advice in love and gentleness. Let us admit our failure in this endeavor and seek God's wisdom and strength for our understanding and success. God's desire for us is to live in community unified by the Holy Spirit for the single purpose of loving one another. Let us remember that no one is without fault and that all are insufficient in godly wisdom. Let us constantly turn to our God and receive His gracious love, mercy, forgiveness, and strength so that we are empowered to support, console, help, counsel, and advise one another in times of difficulty. Let us truly understand what it means to be the body of Christ so that others will take note and perhaps seek God.

Blessedness

Praise be to the God and Father of our Lord Jesus Christ, who has blessed us in the heavenly realms with every spiritual blessing in Christ. For he chose us in him before the creation of the world to be holy and blameless in his sight. In love he predestined us for adoption to sonship through Jesus Christ, in accordance with his pleasure and will—to the praise of his glorious grace, which he has freely given us in the One he loves.

—EPHESIANS 1:3–6 (NIV)

As disciples of our Lord Jesus, we soon discover that the decision to live a life pleasing to God is no small matter. Scripture reveals to us that following the path of Jesus requires us to stop satisfying our own will by giving up control concerning many things. If we imagine ourselves sitting on the hillside near the Sea of Galilee and listening to Jesus describe the many states of blessedness, we soon realize that we have misunderstood the meaning of being blessed. It is only when we decide to follow Jesus as the way, the truth, and the life that we begin to see the truth and understand our desperate need for God's help in changing our ways. Once we allow God's wisdom to sink in, we see that the state of blessedness, the act of receiving divine blessings, is about having an abiding relationship with God and not about the abundance of possessions. We should carefully note that the state of blessedness taught by Jesus, which we call "the beatitudes," has nothing to do with worldly prosperity.

To achieve this blessed state, it is helpful to consider ourselves as pilgrims on a journey to a kingdom unlike any other on earth. Our journey should teach us that a transformation is required for residence in this unusual kingdom. The sovereign Lord and King, Christ Jesus, has expectations that we start to reflect His image in thought, word, and deed. This may require us to suffer the label of fool from our worldly acquaintances when we repent of the past and choose the new, but we should expect little success if our journey is filled only with good intensions and the occasional good work. It is the life devoted to abiding in God through scripture reading, prayer, and community worship and service that renews our minds and empowers us to overcome our misdirected passions. We must enter the path by the narrow gate to find the meaning of life and the way of peace.

Dear disciple, let us humble ourselves and choose the path of Jesus so that we enter the narrow gate of blessedness. Let us receive the wisdom of God and understand that God's kingdom calls us to a life of service, not to lording our greatness over others. Let us not be put off by any perceived hardship in our journey; rather, let us embrace God's transforming work and submit to the Holy Spirit's pruning and refining fire so that we might be born anew. Let us see our impossible debt owed to God, let us receive the magnanimous gift of His grace, and let us proclaim in praise and worship, "I know my redeemer lives!"
(Job 19:25 NKJV).

Those Who Have Gone Before

Therefore, since we are surrounded by such a great cloud of witnesses, let us throw off everything that hinders and the sin that so easily entangles. And let us run with perseverance the race marked out for us, fixing our eyes on Jesus, the pioneer and perfecter of faith. For the joy set before him he endured the cross, scorning its shame, and sat down at the right hand of the throne of God. Consider him who endured such opposition from sinners, so that you will not grow weary and lose heart.

—HEBREWS 12:1–3 (NIV)

As disciples of our Lord Jesus, we should stand in awe of our God, who has given us such a wonderful legacy passed on to us by holy and faithful saints for thousands of years. It may be somewhat overwhelming to compare our lives with those who have completely devoted their lives to God, for the "great cloud of witnesses" stretches from ancient times to the present and represents those who have willingly set their former lives aside to follow in the footsteps of Christ Jesus. Whether prophets of old, apostles, martyrs, church fathers, missionaries, or the countless faithful, these saints renounced their worldly affections and, at times, their dignity and honor to bring glory and honor to God.

These devout Christians allowed their lives to be transformed by

God's covenant love so that they might demonstrate the kingdom of God to anyone who would receive "the good news of Jesus." Despite their outwardly difficult and austere lives, they were strengthened by the rich consolation of the Holy Spirit. In becoming strangers to the world, they became close, intimate friends of God. Despite being despised by the world, they were comforted in knowing that they were precious in God's eyes and that they were greatly loved. Their lives demonstrated true humility and simplicity by being obedient to Jesus's commands to love, to forgive, and to show compassion and mercy for others.

Dear disciple, let us take note and listen carefully to the saints both old and new and receive understanding as to how our lives might validate our claim to being followers of Jesus. Our journey on the path God lays before us should be one of joy and fulfillment, not one filled with envy, complaining, or protest. Let us remember that the saints had a beginning to their journey that required much prayer, scripture study, and fellowship in order to become faithful followers of Jesus. This same path is open to us as well. If we choose to be possessed by the Holy Spirit, we too can experience the power of God's love, forgiveness, and wisdom, allowing us to be transformed into saints capable of demonstrating God's kingdom to others. Let us resolve to reject a lukewarm life characterized as wickedness and laziness. Let us demonstrate our love of Jesus by keeping His commandment "to love as I have loved you" and allow our God to add our names to the great cloud of witnesses.

The Spirit of Discipline

Endure hardship as discipline; God is treating you as his children. For what children are not disciplined by their father? If you are not disciplined—and everyone undergoes discipline—then you are not legitimate, not true sons and daughters at all. Moreover, we have all had human fathers who disciplined us and we respected them for it. How much more should we submit to the Father of spirits and live!

—HEBREWS 12:7–9 (NIV)

As disciples of our Lord Jesus, we must understand the core meaning of our chosen title. To claim the title of disciple means that we have given God complete authority to discipline us by whatever means necessary so that we might become worthy bearers of God's image. With scripture as our guide, we should hear Jesus tell us exactly what it looks like to be His follower; therefore, we, as His disciples, should make discipline and transformation our top priority so that our lives abound in every virtue God has lifted up as good. If we are truly committed to listening to God for understanding, we will quickly see that this transformation is more easily said than done. God reveals to us that the focus of our interior being must change for our exterior actions to reflect the ways of Jesus to others. Each day we must wake up and pray, "Lord Jesus, help me be Your hands and feet in Your holy service. Give me Your wisdom, guidance, and strength to stay on Your path of perfection."

We must be diligent in our commitment and be willing to receive discipline from our God if we are to see any progress toward victory over our selfish wants and desires. Even with our best intentions, we experience frequent failures, which should wake us up to our desperate need for God's help and discipline. We must admit that our ways are not God's ways and should therefore commit ourselves to spending serious time listening during our time of prayer and meditation so that we come to know and embrace the sweetness of God's ways. It is such a sweet moment when we come to know that there is no better consolation than to rest in the arms of God and truly experience divine love and mercy. God becomes real to us as we learn to experience the presence of the Holy Spirit with our senses. "Taste and see that the Lord is good; Blessed is the one who trusts in Him!" (Psalm 34:8 NIV). It is in receiving and trusting that we allow God to transform us into a new creation!

Dear disciple, let us be committed to a habit of morning prayer resolution to be true disciples of Jesus. Let us commit to evening prayer examination to see our successes and failures and ask God's forgiveness and strength for a better tomorrow. Let us be disciplined in scripture reading and faith community sharing so that we experience the overcoming life. Let us be clear about our goal as faithful followers of Jesus so that we live a life pleasing to God. Even though Jesus tells us to "count the cost" (Luke 14:28 NLT), let us see that Jesus's way leads to a life with meaning and purpose. Let us make up our minds to persevere and begin to enjoy our eternal reward today!

The Place of Solitude

But Jesus often withdrew to lonely places and prayed.

—LUKE 5:16 (NIV)

As disciples of our Lord Jesus, have we taken to heart Jesus's example and seen the value of withdrawing to a place of solitude for prayer? The practice of this spiritual discipline deepens our encounters with God and helps us better receive Holy Spirit wisdom and spiritual gifts. In order to develop this intimate relationship with our God, it is essential for us to find a place free from daily distractions and set aside time solely for meditation and silence. We must turn from our usual pursuit of worldly curiosities so that our minds are free to truly receive God's wisdom. For this practice to fully succeed, our minds must be filled with the Word of God for this is the basis God uses to communicate wisdom to us. We must be very specific in our prayer requests concerning the answers needed for kingdom service. We must also learn to stop talking at God and learn to listen in silence for God's answer. Again, God will use scripture to reveal the truth we must hear. For us to hear God, we must know scripture well. It is in this daily practice that we train our minds for godly thought. The resulting transformation of our thinking and reasoning enables and empowers us in discernment as to the things that are pleasing to God. Our usual activities of idle talk, listening to gossip, spreading rumors, and senseless running about will be replaced by loving, compassionate, forgiving action toward everyone we encounter. What joy we experience when we are no longer the center of our universe!

In withdrawing from worldly people and their practices, we are no longer compelled to follow the ways of protest and argument for we now see the truth of God's wisdom. By practicing this spiritual discipline, we come to see the value of humility, for it is in humble service that we find satisfaction and peace. When we begin to know God as much as God can be known and give God all honor and glory, we will be rewarded with the power of the Holy Spirit and enabled to overcome the many temptations to which we are prone: pride, arrogance, envy, lust, covetousness, dishonesty, bias, and prejudice.

Dear disciple, let us ask God to frequently remind us how fleeting are the pleasures of this world. Let us see the sorrowful, destructive path that results from satisfying our sensual cravings and seek the freedom found in the loving, merciful, forgiving embrace of our God. Let us leave vanity to others and become devoted to the way, truth, and life of our Lord Jesus. Let us discover the awe-inspiring wonder found in the presence of our God and learn to listen for God's still small voice that whispers life and blessings of peace and rest for our troubled and weary souls.

A Troubled Heart

When I kept silent, my bones wasted away through my groaning all day long. For day and night your hand was heavy on me; my strength was sapped as in the heat of summer. Then I acknowledged my sin to you and did not cover up my iniquity. I said, "I will confess my transgressions to the Lord." And you forgave the guilt of my sin.

—PSALM 32:3–5 (NIV)

As disciples of our Lord Jesus, we rejoice at hearing the good news concerning the invitation to enter the kingdom of God, but our rejoicing soon fades as we ponder the requirements for entrance. We hear that we are loved and forgiven, but we also hear that we can no longer live unpleasing lives before our God. It is revealed that we are guilty of sin (our human condition) and sins (unpleasing acts) and that we must confess the truth of our condition and repent, that is, turn from our selfish ways and allow God to help us change for the better. Even though this revelation can trouble our hearts, we should hear the good news of Jesus and understand that rescue, our salvation, is close at hand. There may be sorrow and weeping over our condition of lostness, but we must not despair. Distress over these matters may exist for a time, but we must not dwell on our present state. God has provided us with powerful hope, for

Jesus has paved the way with clear teachings for our transformation and redemption. Our rejoicing returns as we choose Jesus to be our defining light, which leads us to a life of meaning and purpose in the kingdom of God.

As disciples, we should consider it pure joy for God to reveal our faults and flaws, for if we choose to live in blind liberty, we will never find true joy and happiness in this life. Joy comes to us as we learn what it means to abide in our God, for it is by dwelling in God's presence with our minds full of scripture that we feel our guilt replaced with a good conscience. Happy are we when we embrace the Holy Spirit and allow God to cast off every stain and burden that oppresses and worries our minds.

Dear disciple, let us learn to trust our God and not allow sorrow and mourning over our failure in thought, word, or deed to consume our thinking, causing us to sink into hopelessness. Let us use every opportunity to practice intimacy with our God for the renewing of our minds. Let us draw close in prayer and meditation, sit still, and listen for the words of God to speak comfort and healing to our troubled and sorrowful hearts. Let us be filled with the Holy Spirit and know that we are loved, that we are forgiven, and that we are part of God's kingdom. Let us take hold of our inheritance and dwell in God's presence so that we experience divine guidance and strength in our times of need.

Misery

If your law had not been my delight, I would have perished in my affliction. I will never forget your precepts, for by them you have preserved my life.

—PSALM 119:92–93 (NIV)

As disciples of our Lord Jesus, we should understand that without God, our lives are doomed to misery. Misery is an unfortunate part of the human condition, a wretched state common to all. Not all seem to suffer equally, but no one is exempt. There is no one on earth who does not suffer the consequences of their sinful condition. Without divine guidance, this unpleasant state can possess and lead our minds into a dark place of despair and hopelessness, but a different perspective is available to the one who chooses to follow the way of Jesus Christ. Our experience speaks loudly to the reality that we need guidance when things take a turn for the worse, so where do we usually go for answers?

When we seek answers to our misery from the world, we may be tempted to look with envy at those who appear to be unaffected because of their wealth or power, but if we seek revelation from God through scripture, we are reminded that our happiness and security are not found in abundant wealth and possessions. These temporal things hold no guarantees and often become burdensome due to their uncertainty. This burden frequently leads to a discontented mind filled with worry and anxiety instead of the consolation of peace and security we seek for our miserable state. Our only relief is found in the pursuit of the spiritual life guided by the presence of our God. Even as we become aware of our corrupt nature, we must cry out more fervently to God for deliverance. It is folly to believe the lies of the worldly who seem to enjoy their miserable and corrupt life. Their love of the cheap and worthless things of the world leads only to sorrow.

Dear disciple, let us rest assured in God and His kingdom and see that this blessed relationship is our only rescue from a life of misery. Let us love the Lord our God with all our being and abide in the presence of the Holy Spirit so that we receive the delights of life. Let us seek the wisdom of Jesus to understand what it means to love our neighbor. Let us experience the blessing of peace as the Holy Spirit teaches us how to offer compassion and good will. Let us receive the necessary gifts of humility and patience from our God so we can overcome our misery. Let us recognize and admit to our own feebleness in this matter and learn to rely on the faithful love and mercy of our God.

Death

"Most assuredly, I say to you, he who hears My word and believes in Him who sent Me has everlasting life, and shall not come into judgment, but has passed from death into life. Most assuredly, I say to you, the hour is coming, and now is, when the dead will hear the voice of the Son of God; and those who hear will live."

—JOHN 5:24–25 (NKJV)

Death is an inescapable fact, but as disciples of our Lord Jesus, how often do we consider our own fate? Daily, our media floods us with stories of death. More personally, we attend funerals for friends and loved ones, but do we pause and consider any urgency for our condition? We have heard the proverbial statement that we should "live each day as if it is our last," but do we consider our purpose for living? It is said that those who have lived well die with a clear conscience and no fear of death, but is this really possible? Only when we are enlightened by the wisdom of God do we understand the fleeting nature of this life and should therefore hold loosely to the things of earth. Knowing and understanding the eternal nature of the kingdom of God should help us grow in our assurance of our inheritance, which strengthens us to be well prepared for death at any moment.

In learning to follow the path of Jesus, we should remember

our temporal condition and consider why we place so much value in living a long life unless our focus changes from worldly gain to things eternal. A life filled with vanity is a dead life full of useless goals. This sad state has nothing to offer when confronted with a troubled, guilty conscience except the delusion that there is all the time in the world to make amends. Only fools trust in reasonable lies for there are no guarantees concerning tomorrow. What consolation remains for anyone facing their end, if spiritual poverty is their only legacy? Their wretched life flashes before their eyes, and they realize that their worldly pursuits, their wealthy and possessions, and their so-called reputation are now worthless. Left are only guilt, regret, and fear for their unknown future.

Dear disciple, let us remain faithful to the path made known to us by our Savior Jesus and commit to His goals and not our own. Let us understand that infusing all of our activities with love shows that we know the difference between being busy for God and being devoted to God. Let us remember that time is precious and that these are the days of our salvation. Let us not put off claiming the gift of eternal life purchased for us by our Lord Jesus so that when we die, we can look forward to hearing His precious words. "Well done, good and faithful servant!"

The Judgment of God

You, therefore, have no excuse, you who pass judgment on someone else, for at whatever point you judge another, you are condemning yourself, because you who pass judgment do the same things. Now we know that God's judgment against those who do such things is based on truth. So when you, a mere human being, pass judgment on them and yet do the same things, do you think you will escape God's judgment? Or do you show contempt for the riches of his kindness, forbearance and patience, not realizing that God's kindness is intended to lead you to repentance? But because of your stubbornness and your unrepentant heart, you are storing up wrath against yourself for the day of God's wrath, when his righteous judgment will be revealed.

—ROMANS 2:1–5 (NIV)

As disciples of our Lord Jesus, we usually hear the word *judgment* used to describe God's displeasure with our disobedience, but do we fully understand the concept surrounding God's judgment? God's judgment, as described in the Old Testament, is concerned with the consequences facing those who refuse to turn from their wicked ways. This is often described as being under the wrath of God as opposed to the condition of those who have chosen to enter a blessed relationship with their God and community. The state of blessedness is also a judgment from God, although we may not see it that way. God's judgment begins in the Garden of Eden, runs all the way to the book of Revelation, and is based on a divine law of justice. Anyone who has been in a court of law knows that justice demands judgment. In view of this fact, why are we so slow to understand our condition before an all-knowing God who accepts no bribes or excuses? We, who are fearful for our reputation before others, should be infinitely more fearful to stand before our Creator! The New Testament authors testify that God's judgment still stands and demands justice. The sooner we understand our helplessness as sinners, the sooner we will cry out for help and mercy before our God. Thanks be to God for Christ Jesus, our Savior, who willingly and lovingly takes up our cause before the Father!

It is good news indeed that Christ Jesus rescues us from the wrath of God. We are no longer lost trying to defend ourselves before a Holy God with good works and self-sacrifices as if we could earn God's favor. As we study scripture, pray continually, and fellowship with our Christian brothers and sisters, we realize that we are no longer alone in our struggle with our guilt and shame. God has enlightened our corrupt way of thinking and empowered us to be more like Jesus. We no longer try to justify ourselves because God has justified us in Christ Jesus and assures us that our hope in an eternal inheritance is true. The result of trusting in the promises of God made clear in scripture is the cleansing of our sin and guilt by the sacrificial blood of Jesus. We are now as white as snow and understand Paul's statement that there is no condemnation for those made one with God through Christ Jesus.

Dear disciple, let us take hold of the gift of salvation so that we have no fear of judgment before our God. Let us rely on the Holy Spirit's wisdom to guide and empower us for life's journey. Let us understand our righteous position before God because of Christ Jesus and give up judging others who struggle and fail before God.

Are we not just as guilty? Let us give all thanks and praise to our God for the multifaceted gift of grace that rescues us, redeems us, and grants us peace of mind in knowing that we need not fear judgment from our Creator.

Devoted to Transformation

Therefore, I urge you, brothers and sisters, in view of God's mercy, to offer your bodies as a living sacrifice, holy and pleasing to God—this is your true and proper worship. Do not conform to the pattern of this world, but be transformed by the renewing of your mind. Then you will be able to test and approve what God's will is—his good, pleasing and perfect will.

—ROMANS 12:1–2 (NIV)

As disciples of our Lord Jesus, we should take careful notice of the influence others have had in guiding us toward moral and ethical values. At an early age, it is made clear that much is expected of us, and so begins our life of anxious uncertainties. Although we may receive the occasional word of praise, we must endure criticism for our failures and often hear things like "Shape up" or "Get your act together." Where do we turn to receive the enabling skills necessary to navigate this life of high expectations? We listen as our learned teachers and elders recommend all sorts of wisdom literature, philosophies, and practices to aid us in self-discovery. When the everyday activities of life fail to satisfy, we may seek the spiritual advice of others, who testify to the benefits of all kinds of religious practices even to extremes, but we, who have heard Jesus's tender call through one of His faithful, now understand the futility of trying to live the life expected of us without God's help. God's divine revelation helps us see our purpose, which requires breaking from our old ways of dealing with the uncertainties of life so that we can move into the overcoming life of discipleship. Jesus tells us, "Do not worry (Matthew 6:25 NIV)," but our first impulse is to think, *That's ridiculous.* How can we not worry when life is so full of uncertainties? But if we are willing to allow our compassionate God free reign in our lives, the Holy Spirit will guide us into a faith community where other disciples can reveal God's answers to our dilemma in a real and tangible way.

Once we devote our lives to following Jesus, we begin to understand what is required for us to have the life we have always wanted and understand that the only way to move forward on Jesus's path is by knowing God intimately. If we pay close attention, God will be proven compassionate and faithful over and over again. This should deepen our faith and help us understand what it means to trust our God in all things. As we experience God's providential care, we should see the wisdom in turning more frequently to God for help and stop trying to be so self-sufficient. What a blessing it is to see our lives slowly transform and actually begin to resemble that of a faithful follower of Jesus. We should stand in awe of our compassionate God who provides comfort and consolation through our faith community when we are assaulted by life's uncertainties.

Dear disciple, the path to complete confidence in God's ways requires much letting go on our part. The spiritual disciplines used by the saints of old show us the tried-and-true way. As Psalm 119 so eloquently tells us, we must know and meditate on God's commands, laws, and precepts until we know them by heart. We must also know the teaching of Jesus and His truths as expounded by the New Testament authors. We must dwell on these truths in God's presence, asking for the Holy Spirit's help in understanding so that we are transformed by the renewing of our minds. Let us never stop meeting with our Christian friends for accountability to our task. Let us commit to freeing ourselves from the anxieties of life's uncertainties by abiding in God through the Holy Spirit for it is here that we taste the sweetness of God's kingdom and find consolations to satisfy our every need.

Meditation

Let the words of my mouth and the meditation of my heart
Be acceptable in Your sight, O Lord, my strength and my Redeemer.

—PSALM 19:14 (NKJV)

Oh, how I love Your law! It is my meditation all the day.

—PSALM 119:97 (NKJV)

I will meditate on the glorious splendor of Your majesty,
And on Your wondrous works.

—PSALM 145:5 (NKJV)

As disciples of our Lord Jesus, we are called to meditate on the things God holds dear. Jesus tells us that "the kingdom of God is near" (Mark 1:15 NLT), but do we fully understand what this means? Many seem to think of the kingdom of God as some remote place in the distant future, but we should see that because of Jesus, the kingdom of God has in fact arrived. What a blessing it is when we understand that God's presence with us establishes God's kingdom. God is our king, Jesus is our Lord, and the Holy

Spirit is God's presence. This is "good news" as we begin to see that "kingdom" benefits are now open to us. This new insight is the key to our growth in the spiritual discipline of meditation. Meditation allows us to encounter God in a real and personal way so that we truly start to see what the kingdom of God is all about. Meditation unlocks the mystery of the abiding presence of God as we encounter the Holy Spirit. Meditation reveals the reality of the power of Jesus in our lives as we become immersed in the love of the Father. This sweet communion with God can be overwhelming as we are embraced with great comfort, joy, and peace. As we grow in the practice of meditation, we will be compelled to incorporate our kingdom enlightenment into all we say and do. Our new vision allows us to see outside of ourselves and embrace our responsibility for the needs of others. We should strive to glorify God, which is to make God tangible to others by our every action.

So how do we practice meditation? Simply sitting quietly while trying to empty our minds in an attempt to hear God speak is nearly impossible. Our minds are easily consumed with cares and desires that push and shove their way into our thinking, allowing the busyness of the world to crush in on us. How are we to deal with this distraction? The answer lies in having an intimate knowledge of God's Holy Word. Having scripture in our mind equips us to receive God's wisdom while we meditate. We start by picturing a biblical setting and then listen to the teachings. We must then ask God to help us understand and wait patiently for God to reveal the answer. We are an impatient lot and must not become discouraged, for answers come slowly at first, but as our knowledge of scripture grows, God will speak more readily. This is the path to enlightenment as we allow God to transform our minds and put a right spirit within us.

Dear disciple, let us commit to daily meditation so that we become vessels fit for God's presence. Let us welcome the Bridegroom so that we become a temple for God's Holy Spirit. Let us constantly invite God's presence and deny entrance to all others. In doing this, we will find the richness of the abiding life promised by our

Lord Jesus, which allows the lure of the world to gradually fade away. Let us remember the brevity of our pilgrimage in the world and the necessity of devout focus on the eternal. By this, we are empowered to overcome and withstand any struggle, suffering, or anxious uncertainty in this life, knowing full well the certainty of our eternal dwelling in the kingdom of God.

Humility Revisited

Good and upright is the Lord; Therefore He teaches sinners in the way. The humble He guides in justice, And the humble He teaches His way. All the paths of the Lord are mercy and truth, To such as keep His covenant and His testimonies.

—PSALM 25:8–10 (NKJV)

As disciples of our Lord Jesus, we must have the mindset of humility in order to receive and implement the divine instruction necessary for living a life pleasing to our God. This requires us to admit that we are prideful and arrogant people who choose our ways over God's. Next, we must allow our minds to be filled with scripture to understand the necessity of humility. We should also appreciate the difficulty of the journey for becoming humble is an arduous task requiring God's help at every turn. The obstacle to our success on the matter of humility is rooted in the belief that our selfish reasoning will somehow guide us into happiness and peace. This attitude erects barriers of resistance to the path of truth even as our way continues to fail, but once we allow the teachings of Jesus to pierce our minds, our conscience becomes convicted and we come to realize the vast difference between our ways and God's. We need God's compassionate and gracious presence to draw us toward the truth so that the Holy Spirit can guide us into right thinking. This happens only when we ask God to put an attitude of humility within us, for humility is actually a gift from God. We must allow God to become part of our every thought. Every morning, we must pray for God to help us understand our need for the Holy Spirit's guidance and strength so that we are empowered to face the humiliation we often encounter and face it well in humility.

In this journey, we should be willing for God to show us that we are not the only ones suffering from pride and arrogance. Everyone suffers from this condition. God's love for us is demonstrated in Jesus, who looks at us with compassion knowing we are all lost sheep in need of a Good Shepherd. Spending time daily with God gives us vision to see as Jesus sees and enlightens us as to why humility is essential for the Christian life. As God lifts us out of our humiliation, we begin to see that the humble life is a life of power. When we allow God to make us a proper dwelling place for the Holy Spirit, we are freed more and more from our selfish, prideful ways. When we choose to take on Jesus's humility, we are enabled to abide in our God in a most powerful way, resulting in our being filled with a sense of love and peace. As humble followers of Jesus, we are then empowered to love and console others as Jesus loves and consoles us.

Dear disciple, even as we devote our lives to humble service in God's kingdom, we will continue to face humiliation from others as they try to shame us into submission to their will, so it is essential to remain firmly established in God's presence; otherwise, our old selves will rise up to flex prideful arrogance. Let us commit to overcoming our weakness and refuse to depend on our own ways. Let us devote ourselves to the humble path of God so that we receive guidance in the midst of our many vexations. Let us stop being obsessed over what others think of us and learn to value God's vision for us. Let us place our security in God's presence and receive the Holy Spirit's guiding and enabling power so that we become blessed to be faithful, humble servants.

Peace of Mind

"All this I have spoken while still with you. But the Advocate, the Holy Spirit, whom the Father will send in my name, will teach you all things and will remind you of everything I have said to you. Peace I leave with you; my peace I give you. I do not give to you as the world gives. Do not let your hearts be troubled and do not be afraid."

—JOHN 14:25–27 (NIV)

As disciples of our Lord Jesus, we must understand that true peace of mind comes only from complete trust in God. The consequence of receiving this blessed gift of peace is a greater capacity to do good in the world. God's good will becomes our desire as we let go of our worldly passions that turn our minds toward shameful things. We understand that the peace of God empowers us to obey Jesus's command "Do not worry about tomorrow" (Matthew 6:34 NIV). What joy we experience when we are no longer obsessed with the uncertainties of life, which bring only worry and anxiety. What a blessing it is to feel the consoling and assuring touch of God even as we are assaulted by the slander and lies of others.

We often witness the many disturbed and discontented of the world who are never at peace and who disrupt the peace for anyone near them. They blather on about irrelevant things leaving tension and strife in their wake all the while refusing the healing ways of

God. The discontented are consumed with complaining about the shortcomings of others while leaving their own faults intact. With so many bad examples before us, why are we so slow in directing the zeal of correction upon ourselves? Shouldn't we stop rationalizing our own sinful actions with excuses? Shouldn't we look in God's mirror and plead guilty? We must allow the truth of God to clear our minds so that we see clearly our desperate need of a Savior! We must wake up and see that we are all imperfect and therefore bear with each other's failures. Our God is compassionate and gracious. Are we not called to do the same? Humility is the path to peace of mind whereby we should be quick to offer charity rather than ugliness. Our only protection from a vulgar, petty, and angry spirit is to be one with God through Jesus Christ and the Holy Spirit.

Dear disciple, we cannot achieve peace of mind without God. It is God who makes us capable of being holy, which frees us to be charitable in all circumstances. By abiding in our God, we are enabled to live at peace with harsh and perverse people who irritate us to no end. Let us receive the grace of God that saves us from ourselves, so that we receive consolation from the Holy Spirit in our times of stress. Let us not be troubled by the burdensome actions of others and allow God's glory to flow through us. Although this life may be full of misery and uncertainty, we of God must be committed to the overcoming life found in Jesus Christ. This is where we find the assurance of our heavenly treasures, which gives us peace of mind amid all of life's uncertainties.

Burdens

"Come to me, all you who are weary and burdened, and I will give you rest. Take my yoke upon you and learn from me, for I am gentle and humble in heart, and you will find rest for your souls. For my yoke is easy and my burden is light."

—MATTHEW 11:28–30 (NIV)

As disciples of our Lord Jesus, our desire must be focused on two things in order to cast off our burdens and drawer closer to God: simplicity in life and purity of heart. A life of simplicity removes many worldly obstacles that weigh us down and hinder our abiding with God. By accepting the yoke of Jesus, we embrace the presence of the Holy Spirit and begin to enjoy the consolations of God as our hearts are purified from our sins. If our hearts are free from the burden of selfish desires and worries, good will for our neighbor will come easily for us. If our sole aim is to seek nothing but the pleasure of God, we will enjoy the ability to love others as God loves us. If we are someone with a heart for God, we will see the world as God sees it. As we become purified in God's presence, we will see the godly purpose of things clearly and be empowered to use them unselfishly. The truth of God's purpose for us will penetrate our formerly stubborn minds, allowing us to find more and more ways to love God and neighbor.

True joy is given only to those who choose to cast off their burdens and let their hearts become purified by the abiding presence of God. It is by yoking ourselves to Jesus that we receive godly wisdom and power to overcome our worldly passions. Our vision is no longer blinded by an evil conscience that is ignorant of God, for a mind that continues to pursue selfish satisfaction remains burdened with anguish and affliction. The devout disciple understands full well Jesus's teaching concerning baptism by the Holy Spirit and by fire. We watch with fascination as a blacksmith puts iron into the furnace. As the metal glows white, all traces of rust and impurity are removed, and so it is with the one who turns completely to God and allows the Holy Spirit to strip off our laziness and indifference. The old is gone; the new has come!

Dear disciple, we must be on constant guard against removing the yoke of Jesus and allowing the old self to guide us into laxity and selfish comfort. Let us be honest with ourselves and proclaim that we are weak and in constant need of supervision. Let us cry out, "Help me, Lord Jesus!" Let us become one with our God and claim the victory Jesus has won for us. Let us come to Jesus and accept His yoke of guidance so that we may walk bravely in the ways of God. Let us give up our burdens and our weary ways and start loving one another as Jesus loves us.

Truth about Ourselves

Trust in the Lord with all your heart and lean not on your own understanding; in all your ways submit to him, and he will make your paths straight. Do not be wise in your own eyes; fear the Lord and shun evil.

—PROVERBS 3:5–7 (NIV)

As disciples of our Lord Jesus, we should understand that relying solely on our reasoning ability to guide our lives leads us away from the truth we so desperately need. Scripture is clear concerning our fate if we choose our ways over God's. Our conscience is supposed to be our guide, but when we neglect turning to God for guidance in all matters of life, we risk becoming hardened against God's ways as we depend more and more on the ways of the world. We must admit that we are blind to our selfish and critical nature and find any excuse to justify ourselves. Our wicked actions are spurred on by an attitude of superiority, which allows our unbridled, self-seeking passions to ignore the plight of others. Our cutting words wound as we judge the faults and failures of others while never considering our own shortcomings. We cultivate relationships with those who look, act, and think like we do while shunning all others.

If we claim to be followers of Jesus, we should know that our lives are but folly and vanity without God. We should be constantly running from the darkness of the world into the light of Jesus, our guide to the way, truth, and life found only in God's kingdom. Unless God's guiding hand rests upon us, we have little capacity for compassion and grace. We take others to task for the smallest mistakes while overlooking our great sins. It seems others can do no right while we can do no wrong. Let us give thanks to our God, who is compassionate, gracious, and long-suffering for us. Let us give thanks to saintly friends who love and encourage us to pursue God more closely. Let us give thanks for the wisdom of God that opens our minds to the ways of Jesus and the joy-filled life, even in times of trouble.

Dear disciple, true happiness in life comes only when we let God transform us into the likeness of Jesus. When we allow our conscience to be guided by the Holy Spirit, we are less easily affected by the ever-present disturbing affairs of the world. We become less concerned with gossiping about others and focus more on overcoming our own faults. Spending time with and learning to trust God empowers us to let go of our temporal cares. The words of Jesus should remind us daily to place God above all else. Let us commit to the path of perfection laid before us by our God so that we receive blessing upon blessing and in turn become a blessing to others.

Having a Clear Conscience

The goal of this command is love, which comes from a pure heart and a good conscience and a sincere faith. Some have departed from these and have turned to meaningless talk. They want to be teachers of the law, but they do not know what they are talking about or what they so confidently affirm.

—1 TIMOTHY 1:5–7 (NIV)

As disciples of our Lord Jesus, we must endure a great deal of purification in order to see the world rightly. We must gain understanding in order to address the age-old questions concerning the meaning of good and evil, right and wrong. Many would point to something we call our conscience as the source that shapes our decisions concerning these questions, but what is it that guides the workings of our conscience? As we grow up, we are taught many things from many sources that have shaped who we are, but unless God's truth permeates our minds, we are ill equipped to make good judgments concerning what is good or right in life. Godly wisdom is essential for rightly guiding us in all matters of life, whether they be thought, word, or deed.

We are taught that as sinners, we can never experience true inner joy or peace as long as we continue to allow our selfish motives free reign as guidance counselors. The prophet Isaiah said, "There is no peace for the wicked" (Isaiah 48:22 NIV), so shouldn't we recognize our dilemma and allow our Lord and Savior Jesus the Christ free reign in cleaning and correcting our conscience? When we draw close to God in prayer, scripture study, and fellowship with Christian friends, the Holy Spirit should fill us with assurance that "with God, all things are possible" (Matthew 19:26 NIV). Those with a "good conscience" give testimony to having experienced God's purifying presence in this way. Their lives rightly show the power of God's love that gives a great capacity for happiness and the ability to bring joy to others even while bearing adversity.

Why would we choose to suffer an evil conscience when the answer lies clearly before us? Do we enjoy enduring anxious thoughts and worries caused by a mind contaminated by the influence of an ever-present evil world? Are we just too busy or just too lazy to involve God in our lives? How sad it is when we become so self-absorbed with our own agendas that we choose not to take the time to know our God and the path of righteousness, which frees our conscience for good.

Dear disciple, Paul speaks of a "renewed mind" that is no longer occupied with excuses for selfish behavior, broken relationships, and a multitude of worries. The mind possessed by God seeks only God's glory, which allows us to show the reality of God to others. Let us devote ourselves to a humble mindset and receive Holy Spirit power to love and forgive as Jesus. Let us see as Jesus sees so that our every deed is driven toward compassion, justice, and mercy. Let us seek and embrace our God and receive a good conscience to guide us in all we say and do! Let us fulfill the purpose for which we were created, which is to love our God with all our heart, mind, and strength and be reborn with a clear conscience that enables us to live in blessed relationships of love for one another.

Blessedness of Loving Jesus

While Jesus was having dinner at Matthew's house, many tax collectors and sinners came and ate with him and his disciples. When the Pharisees saw this, they asked his disciples, "Why does your teacher eat with tax collectors and sinners?" On hearing this, Jesus said, "It is not the healthy who need a doctor, but the sick. But go and learn what this means: 'I desire mercy, not sacrifice.' For I have not come to call the righteous, but sinners."

—MATTHEW 9:10–13 (NIV)

As disciples of our Lord Jesus, we joyfully testify that our condition as sinners is not hopeless because the "good news" of Jesus proclaims that forgiveness and healing are open to all. This is the state of blessedness that results from choosing to become a committed follower of Jesus. Blessedness is feeling God's loving touch that invites us into an intimate relationship. When we begin loving God above of all created things, we see the path to freedom from the sin that entangles us with selfish misery. God's divine revelation opens our minds to understand that our affection for temporal things or our trust in the worldly ways of people fails to satisfy our longings and can leave us disillusioned and cynical. Our clinging to the frail things of this world leaves us feeling unfulfilled and so disappointed. Isn't it time for us to embrace the loving and trusting arms of Jesus and be empowered for this life and ultimately to eternal life? Only our God can give us help and strength in our time of need. Unlike others, Jesus will never leave us or forsake us, so we should keep Him as our constant companion and consult Him frequently for guidance in all circumstances.

In the busyness of our lives, it is easy to overlook or ignore the peril we constantly face from temptations. In fact, we are in mortal danger the moment we take our eyes off Jesus. Moses, inspired by God, is right to call us stiff-necked people who are slow to repentance. We are quick to say yes to Jesus one moment and then turn back to pursue the lusts of our heart in the next. If our devotion to God consists in brief pauses for momentary prayers and study, we remain the fools thinking we are safe from temptations. Without the blessedness of God's grace, we are doomed to continue down paths of darkness. Do we really want to remain victims of temptation and be drawn into the path toward sinful satisfaction? We gain peace of mind only by seeking the blessed comfort found in the arms of Jesus that protect us from ruin.

Dear disciple, let us learn our lessons quickly and choose the love of Jesus above all else. Let us faithfully seek God's wisdom and enter the life of blessedness for guidance into acts of love. Let us choose to belong wholly to Jesus and cling to Jesus for life. Let us forsake all other paths that lead to sorrow. What joy we receive in knowing that love is understood only in the presence of God! Let us first understand how much we are loved by God and then allow God to free us to truly love one another. Let us pray for the blessedness of godly vision and be empowered to love as the body of Christ.

Why Choose Jesus?

> *"The Spirit of the Lord is on me, because he has anointed me to proclaim good news to the poor. He has sent me to proclaim freedom for the prisoners and recovery of sight for the blind, to set the oppressed free, to proclaim the year of the Lord's favor."*
>
> —LUKE 4:18–19 (NIV)

As disciples of our Lord Jesus, we should frequently meditate on the benefits of an intimate friendship with our Savior. A careful reading of scripture clearly tells us that if we chose to closely follow Jesus, we receive a loving touch like no other that has the power to transform our lives for service in God's kingdom. This should prompt us to ask, "What is my motive in following Jesus?" When we look at the multitude that first followed Jesus, it appears that most followed for selfish reasons, such as physical healing or a free lunch without any consideration for life transformation. But when Jesus challenged their way of life, they quickly fell away, unlike Jesus's true disciples who continued to follow in order to receive something eternal. They listened to Jesus proclaim God's wisdom and saw Him live out this wisdom in acts of compassion, mercy, and forgiveness. These faithful followers truly saw what it meant to do God's will. They were given a supernatural power they had never experienced to deal with the difficulties of life. They were given clarity as to where their allegiance should lie, as to who was really king, as to who was the true source of joy, as to how to overcome selfishness and greed, as to who deserves forgiveness, as to how to pray, as to how to repent, and as to how to understand God as a real presence that could always be trusted.

Those who do not know Jesus do not understand the poverty of their lives, but we who have encountered Jesus know full well the consequences of His absence. Jesus's presence brings peace of mind in hard times, comfort during sorrow, encouragement during failure, and love during times of abandonment. Life is good while living in an oasis, but unless we cling tightly to Jesus, life can become a desert of desperation at a moment's notice. In fact, life without the constant presence of Jesus can quickly become filled with burdens to the point of hopelessness. Our only hope in this life is to fall into the arms of our Savior and Redeemer and receive God's gracious gift of love and Holy Spirit power.

Dear disciple, let us admit that we are weak apart from God. Our feelings are so easily hurt, our pride punctured with the slightest prick, and our cleaver reasoning dashed to the ground with the simplest question. Let us be honest with ourselves and admit that we need help; we need a Savior! With the voice of God calling loudly to us from scripture and with all the testimony of the saints who have gone before pleading with us, let us embrace the fact that life without Jesus results only in disappointment and disaster. Let us come to our senses and know how desperately we need Jesus. Let us commit to making Jesus our most intimate friend, and let us vow to remain close to Jesus in good times and even closer in the bad.

When God Seems Far Away

My God, my God, why have you forsaken me? Why are you so far from saving me, so far from my cries of anguish? My God, I cry out by day, but you do not answer, by night, but I find no rest.

—PSALM 22:1–2 (NIV)

As disciples of our Lord Jesus, we find it easy to be grateful when God's comforting presence is near, but how do we respond when God's gracious hand seems absent? As we grow in our faith, we can readily testify that God's presence in our lives brings us comfort and strength to endure life's hardships and overcome the temptations that so easily entangle us. We might also testify that our cheery disposition, despite our situation, comes from being possessed by God's Holy Spirit. We might go on to say that God's presence frees us to enjoy and cherish family, friends, and all of God's creation, but there are times when even the most devout disciple experiences the absence of God's consolation. This unpleasant journey into darkness should not surprise anyone familiar with God's ways. John of the cross describes this seeming absence of God as the "Dark Night of the Soul," a time for testing our faith and for training in patience and obedience as we wait on our God to act in our best interest.

We must understand that our battle against the lure of the world and our selfish desires never ends and requires God's intervention if we are to move forward in our goal to reach perfection in Jesus. Our path to success is frequently blocked by our refusal to give up our self-sufficiency and turn our trust completely toward God. Our stubbornness allows darkness to enter when troubles arise, and our confused minds force us into survival mode thinking. We become entirely focused on self and are blinded to our need for help from God and our faith community. It seems we never get over feeling shame or embarrassment because of our failures, and we struggle to see that our trials and tribulations are opportunities to draw closer to our God and to grow our faith. It is natural to turn back to our old ways and seek familiar worldly comforts, for this is what we know best, but our loving God desires something better for us. The ways of Jesus, which are infinitely better than our own, are designed to draw us out of our darkness into God's wonderful light, if only we would allow the Holy Spirit to heal our blindness. When darkness comes upon us, we must recognize it as a sign of stubbornness on our part for refusing to continue on the holy path to perfection. Once we see the error of our ways and turn back to God in prayer and community service, we will eventually be consoled by the gracious, loving touch of our God.

Dear disciple, let us confess that our arrogance often leads us into a false sense of security that blinds us to our sin. Our "I've got this" attitude quickly crumbles when we are blindsided by a crisis. Let us recognize this as a spiritual reality check from our God that reminds us to stop taking our Savior Jesus for granted. Even if we believe that trials in life are not our fault, God has ordained them to show us the way of humility and our need for God's help in all things! No one escapes despair, so let us keep our eyes fixed on Jesus and take comfort in the apostle Paul's words. "Thanks be to God, who gives us victory over sin and death through our Lord Jesus Christ" (1 Corinthians 15:57 NKJV).

Gratitude for God's Grace

Let the peace of Christ rule in your hearts, since as members of one body you were called to peace. And be thankful. Let the message of Christ dwell among you richly as you teach and admonish one another with all wisdom through psalms, hymns, and songs from the Spirit, singing to God with gratitude in your hearts. And whatever you do, whether in word or deed, do it all in the name of the Lord Jesus, giving thanks to God the Father through him.

—COLOSSIANS 3:15–17 (NIV)

As disciples of our Lord Jesus, we should constantly give thanks to God for His marvelous grace, but in reality, how often do we bow down before our Creator and Sovereign God with humble and grateful hearts? Are we still guilty of saying, "Look at me and all the great things I have done for God. Am I not a great Christian?" Instead, shouldn't we allow Jesus to lead us in His righteous path so that we see ourselves for who we are and resign ourselves to patiently carry our cross toward the goal of Christian perfection? Our attitude should be one of a humble servant and not of a privileged king! With grateful hearts, we should bask in the grace of God so that we receive discernment as to the difference between God's comfort and worldly comfort. Unless we see that bodily pleasure brings only temporary satisfaction, we will fail to appreciate the magnitude of

God's gracious comfort, in which God infuses the Holy Spirit into our minds as a soothing balm for our troubled souls.

Unless we take hold of God's gracious gift, we will remain prideful and arrogant and continue to suffer the consequences of a sin-stained conscience. We must remain vigilant to the weakness of our human condition and rely wholly on God's gracious presence at all times. Our attitude should be a posture of gratitude giving God thanks and praise for the unmerited gift of divine grace no matter our circumstances. As we receive godly wisdom and practice the ways of Jesus, we are gradually convicted of the fact that, apart from God, we have little if any capacity to do any good thing for God's kingdom. We should admit our poverty and weakness and give thanks to God for every ability we have received. We should recognize that we are to become God's true image bearers whose purpose is to build up the kingdom of God with grateful hearts full of love.

Dear disciple, let us allow God's grace to transform us into grateful, humble servants who no longer feel unappreciated while serving as the least of these. Jesus has promised a special place in His kingdom for those who appear to be last. The saints of old testify to the greatness found in humility before both God and humankind. Let us take notice and appreciate every gift we receive from God and give our God all thanks and praise. Our lives can be difficult at times, but there is no place for a bitter or ungrateful heart in God's kingdom. Even though we are allowed to experience both good and bad, we must remember that God's mysterious ways are for our welfare. Jesus said that the gateway to God's kingdom is narrow and the road is difficult. Let us be grateful that we are not alone in our journey that leads to eternal life.

Discipline for Transformation

Know then in your heart that as a man disciplines his son, so the Lord your God disciplines you. Observe the commands of the Lord your God, walking in obedience to him and revering him.

—DEUTERONOMY 8:5–6 (NIV)

People who accept discipline are on the pathway to life, but those who ignore correction will go astray.

—PROVERBS 10:17 (NLT)

According to Jesus, the kingdom of God is entered through the narrow gate, but are we willing to bear the cross of discipline necessary to enter? As disciples of our Lord Jesus, we eagerly receive God's consolation but are quick to object when we have to endure the trials necessary to reshape us. We love sharing Jesus's table but refuse to partake in His fasting. We readily receive Holy Communion but waver at the sacrifice it implies. We love praise and bless Jesus as long as happiness flows but grumble and complain when hardship comes, thinking Jesus has deserted us. We all desire to be happy in Jesus, but few are willing to suffer anything for Him. Are we not shallow Christians if we only seek to be consoled by our God? Do we really love Jesus if we only think of selfish profit and gain? Are we willing to serve God simply out of love? Is there anyone so godly that they have stripped themselves of all self-interest and human desire? Only those who abandon themselves to God find the true meaning of being born from above.

Those who truly love and know Jesus experience a mind-altering transformation and understand the necessity of discipline through trials for Christian formation. They turn to Jesus and bless Him in times of trial and anguish as well as in times of comfort and rest. We, as followers of Jesus, should never stop giving God thanks and praise no matter our lot, for we know that God disciplines us out of love. We understand that the loving power of discipline frees us from our obsessive selfish interest that causes us to stumble. We are empowered to see as Jesus sees and understand that wealth and knowledge in and of themselves are nothing unless God guides us in their use. When we receive godly wisdom and embrace the Holy Spirit, we are empowered for repentance, devotion, good will, generosity, and good works by renouncing the right to satisfy our worldly desires. We must give up the right to self-glory in order to succeed in following the way of Jesus and should readily proclaim that we are now doing only what we ought to have done all along.

Dear disciple, let us resolve to take up our cross and allow the truth of Christ to permeate our being through and through. There is no other way to enter and thrive in the kingdom of God than to embrace the ways of Jesus. Even though bearing a cross of discipline is difficult, let us remember that we do not bear our cross alone. Let us understand that no one is wealthier, more powerful, or freer than the one who knows the blessings of leaving all former ways behind by choosing to become yoked with Jesus. Let us embrace the attitude of humility by seeing that serving as "the least of these" brings the most blessed gift of God: peace of mind.

The Royal Way of the Cross

Then Jesus said to his disciples, "Whoever wants to be my disciple must deny themselves and take up their cross and follow me. For whoever wants to save their life will lose it, but whoever loses their life for me will find it. What good will it be for someone to gain the whole world, yet forfeit their soul? Or what can anyone give in exchange for their soul?"

—MATTHEW 16:24–26 (NIV)

As disciples of our Lord Jesus, we encounter many teachings from God as we journey through the Bible, some wonderful and some distressing. We love hearing Jesus talk about love, compassion, and forgiveness, but when Jesus says, "Deny yourself, take up your cross and follow me" (Matthew 16:24 NIV) or "Get away from me breaker of God's laws for I never knew you" (Matthew 7:23 NLT), we cringe at the harshness of the message. But once the truth of scripture is revealed to us, we begin to see that Jesus's first statement concerning carrying our cross is the solution to the second statement concerning our sinful human condition. Taking up the cross sounds so hard, but in actuality, it is just another way of saying yes to Jesus's invitation. "Follow Me" (Mark 1:17 NRSV). At first, the way of the cross is difficult and may feel like punishment as we begin to turn away from all the darling lusts we hold so dear. Our rigid self shouts back at us,

"What are you doing?" It seems that temptations are around every corner, calling us back to our old ways. Our only rescue is to stay close to Jesus in prayer and meditation, for the presence of the Holy Spirit is our salvation. We must study God's Word daily and talk to our brothers and sisters in Christ in times of weakness. We must face the cross, prostrate ourselves, plead for forgiveness and mercy, and ask Jesus to help us every moment of every day. We must be honest with ourselves and admit our weaknesses, pick up our crosses, and carry them willingly, knowing that this is the only way to overcome our selfish ways.

The way of the cross is God's solution to our fear of judgment. The way of the cross opens our hearts and minds to the life of Jesus and His miraculous healing and loving power. Our cross becomes our everything and is the necessary refiner's fire we need in order to become completely obedient to the will of God. Our cross gives us discernment as to the truth concerning things temporal and things eternal that lead us to life and true inner peace. It is through the cross that we are born anew. The cross prepares us and enables us to endure the trials and suffering of this world. The cross empowers us to resist worry, fear, envy, gossip, and complaining. The cross reminds us that all glory and honor belong to God alone.

Dear disciple, let us embrace our cross so that we might enter the kingdom of God with confidence and experience paradise on earth in the here and now. Let us pick up our cross with joy so that we enjoy the consolations of God today. Let us kneel before the cross of Jesus and receive our cross of freedom so that we experience the sweetness of Jesus's words of love and comfort in our times of need. What a blessing it is to know and trust the ways of God that form us into a new creation worthy of hearing Jesus's words "Well done, good and faithful servant" (Matthew 25:21 NIV).

Hearing God through Scripture

Blessed is the one who does not walk in step with the wicked or stand in the way that sinners take or sit in the company of mockers, but whose delight is in the law of the Lord, and who meditates on his law day and night. That person is like a tree planted by streams of water, which yields its fruit in season and whose leaf does not wither—whatever they do prospers.

—PSALM 1:1–3 (NIV)

As disciples of our Lord Jesus, we are encouraged to fill our minds with scripture so that we are well equipped to have inward conversations with God. Our time with God in prayer gives us wisdom to understand that the primary purpose of prayer is to listen and receive the divine truth of God. The devout disciple understands full well what the psalmist means in saying, "I will hear what God the LORD will speak, For He will speak peace to His people and to His saints; But let them not turn back to folly" (Psalm 85:8 NKJV). This is the meaning of blessedness: the receiving of God's transforming words of consolation found only by dwelling in the awesome presence of our Creator.

Blessed are the ears that hear and discern the guidance from the divine whisperings found in scripture while shutting out the murmurings of the world. Blessed indeed are the ears that listen to

God's truth that wells up as presence of the Holy Spirit guides us into truth. Blessed are the eyes that are closed to the temptations of the world and open to the revealed glory found in God's Word. Blessed are we who turn daily to Jesus, our Lord and Savior, and continually ask for understanding concerning the divine mysteries of scripture, not that they be explained but believed. Blessed are we who long to spend time with our God in order to cut ourselves off from the snares of temptation.

Dear disciple, let us listen to God's call through scripture and take the path of Jesus so clearly laid out for us so that we can be empowered to rein in our passionate senses. Let us stop our busyness and hear what the Lord our God would say to us today. Our Bridegroom and Beloved says to us, "I am your salvation; I am your peace and your life." Therefore, let us fill our minds with God's Word by abiding in Jesus so that we find rest for our troubled and weary souls. Let us seek that which is eternal and shun that which is temporal. It is our God who will give us understanding in our time of need and open our eyes to the path of righteousness. Humankind may give us temporary aid, but it is our Creator who gives us everlasting joy. Let us exchange our worldly and chaotic ways of thinking and receive the mind of Christ. Let us be led by the Word of God and give the Holy Spirit freedom to transform us into a pleasing aroma for the benefit of all we encounter.

Listening for Understanding

The Lord came and stood there, calling as at the other times, "Samuel! Samuel!" Then Samuel said, "Speak, for your servant is listening."

—1 SAMUEL 3:10 (NIV)

Turn my heart toward your statutes and not toward selfish gain. Turn my eyes away from worthless things; preserve my life according to your word.

—PSALM 119:36–37 (NIV)

Despite being disciples of our Lord Jesus, our minds continue to be consumed by doubts and fears concerning the problems and uncertainties of life. Instead of listening for God's wisdom, we often turn to resources other than God for advice. We seek so-called experts in the hope of finding guidance but are often frustrated when we find no quick fixes for our dilemmas. When we choose to turn back to God, we encounter difficult truths concerning our problems, for they reveal that the root of our problems is our unwillingness to listen. God calls to us through scripture, through the faith community, and through the Holy Spirit, but few seem to hear. Jesus tells the parable of the sower to illustrate an amazing transformation for those who receive the Word of God and are obedient to God's commandments as opposed to those who refuse to listen, those who abandon God's teachings after a brief trial, or those who fail to fully live into God's divine truth. If we want to mature as Christians, we must choose to stop being like the Israelites who gave lip service to God while doing what seemed right in their own eyes and be like Samuel who said, "Speak, for your servant is listening" (1 Samuel 3:10 NIV).

As followers of our Lord Jesus, we should understand that even though doubts and fears continue to come, we will always find comfort and guidance by abiding in the presence of God. We must also understand that God's inspired Word, though very necessary, does not impart God's Spirit. These beautiful words cannot inflame the heart by themselves. They deliver the message of salvation and reconciliation, but only the presence of God can lay bare the soul. Scripture places mysteries before us, but only God can unlock their meaning. These sacred words proclaim God's commandments, but only God through the Holy Spirit can empower us to keep them. The Word of God points the way; God's presence gives us strength for the journey. Scripture directs us toward the path forward; God's Holy Spirit imparts wisdom, which enlightens the heart.

Dear disciple, let us hear the Holy Scripture cry out to us, then let us kneel before our God and receive divine revelation. Let us grasp fully that God's everlasting truth is received only by the presence of the Holy Spirit. Let us, like Peter, embrace Jesus and say, "Lord, to whom shall we go? You have the words of eternal life." Let us cling to the Holy Spirit and plead, "Turn my eyes from worthless things, and give me life through Your truth."

Listening with Humility

When pride comes, then comes disgrace, but with humility comes wisdom.

—PROVERBS 11:2 (NIV)

As disciples of our Lord Jesus, we must learn the benefits of listening with humility as we read scripture, but what should we expect to hear? When we learn to devote ourselves to the path of humility, we begin to hear the sweetness of Jesus's voice calling us to abandon all pretense of wisdom and to sit in devotion and receive all that the Holy Spirit would reveal. The knowledge of great philosophers pales in comparison to the divine words of Jesus that whisper, "My child, my words are spirit and life. Receive them in faith and be reborn. Do not confuse my words with the wisdom of man, which is tainted with vanity" (John 6:63 NIV).

From the beginning, God has called prophets to speak divine words of truth and life to anyone who would consider the path of humility. Unfortunately, so many are hard-hearted and deaf to God's voice and prefer the voice of worldly masters. The truth of the matter is most people prefer listening to promises that satisfy fleshy appetites rather than the eternal promises of God. It seems that they have more confidence in the familiar but fleeting ways of the world than in the ways of a Creator God they cannot see. What would happen if everyone served God with as much passion and energy as they serve the world and its masters? It's amazing how the dull of heart will travel great distances for little gain but scarcely lift a finger for eternal life. They work day and night for empty promises and petty rewards while shunning God's peace and an everlasting inheritance.

Dear disciple, let us rejoice in God's gift of humility so that in listening, we might receive God's divine wisdom. Let us pray for those lost and complaining souls who prefer darkness to light and revel more in vanity than in truth. Let us allow God to write words of truth on our hearts so that we can meditate on them continuously, for they are our fortress in times of trial and temptation. Let us resolve to not give up when God's message is difficult but cry, "Help me understand and receive Your wisdom." Let us understand that God uses difficult life situations and temptations to draw us close in order to strengthen our faith. It is our responsibility to be well trained in God's ways if we hope to succeed in the overcoming life. Let us, therefore, invite the presence of the Holy Spirit and humbly accept the Word of God. Our God is faithful and true and will always console us with unfailing love and guidance as long as we seek and listen with humility.

Walking in God's Truth

Jesus answered, "I am the way and the truth and the life. No one comes to the Father except through me. If you really know me, you will know my Father as well. From now on, you do know him and have seen him." Philip said, "Lord, show us the Father and that will be enough for us." Jesus answered: "Don't you know me, Philip, even after I have been among you such a long time? Anyone who has seen me has seen the Father. How can you say, 'Show us the Father'?"

—JOHN 14:6–9 (NIV)

As disciples of our Lord Jesus, we should understand how critical it is for us to abide in our Triune God in order to succeed in our journey toward Christian perfection. Perhaps the most important aspect of abiding is listening for God's Word, for this is how we receive God's truth for transformation, but do we hear Jesus tell us that in order to receive and understand God's truth, we must become like little children? We may object to this teaching by wondering what is so special about a child's point of view. After all, we see children as stubborn and disobedient, but Jesus sees them as those who see God's creation with awe and wonder. We, on the other hand, must admit that we allow the busyness of our lives to crowd out our wonder of creation. Children are vulnerable for they rely on others for provision, protection, and guidance in order to live. We are prideful and stubborn and find it hard to admit that we need help. We also have trust and control issues, which makes it difficult for us to rely completely on God's gracious gifts. For us to move forward on the path of righteousness, we must understand the meaning of walking in God's truth. Jesus implores us to wake up and adopt a childlike view of God and creation for only then will we understand and experience the abiding presence of God, which empowers us to withstand the seductive attacks from an evil and wicked world. We must allow our God to fill our minds with divine truth if we are ever to be freed for faithful service in God's kingdom.

We must never forget that we are sinners and will always be subject to the entanglement of our passions. Without Jesus, we are quickly overcome with troubles, worries, and fears. We must look often to God's image and see clearly what is pleasing and eternal. We must let go of our worldly curiosity and arrogance that twists God's truth for our selfish gain. Faith allows us to place our trust in God and to stop rationalizing divine mystery for there is no profit toward perfection in this vain exercise. God reveals divine truth only to those who trust fully in God's covenant of love and promise of reconciliation. We must never put our trust in books and outward signs alone. We must no longer be like those who have God on their lips but little of God in their hearts. We must allow our assurance to grow by the presence of the Holy Spirit so that all of our passionate longings are satisfied in God alone.

Dear disciple, let us stop allowing our minds to be compromised by the next great teaching of humankind and pray, "Oh Lord, I am so weak. Let Your truth be my truth. Teach me, guard me, and guide me in Your path. Free me from all evil distractions and disordered love so that I might walk in Your freedom. Help me do what is right and pleasing in Your sight." Let us learn with childlike faith as we abide in our God and experience the life for which we were created. The way, truth, and life of Jesus can be ours if only we will learn to practice the presence of our God.

Divine Love

Whoever confesses that Jesus is the Son of God, God abides in him, and he in God. And we have known and believed the love that God has for us. God is love, and he who abides in love abides in God, and God in him. Love has been perfected among us in this: that we may have boldness in the day of judgment; because as He is, so are we in this world. There is no fear in love; but perfect love casts out fear, because fear involves torment. But he who fears has not been made perfect in love. We love Him because He first loved us.

—1 JOHN 4:15–19 (NKJV)

As disciples of our Lord Jesus, one of the biggest challenges we face is to understand divine love. Our understanding of love is so polluted by our selfish quest to satisfy our passions that it takes the loving power of our Heavenly Father, our Lord Jesus the Christ, and the Holy Spirit to break through our blindness and draw us near. It takes us a while to recognize the difference between our selfish human way of loving and the extravagant agape love demonstrated by our Creator God. The point at which we appreciate the fact that our loving God would condescend to rescue us poor sinning creatures can be quite overwhelming. If we drop our guard and accept our Savior's invitation, we will slowly begin to realize that we have been invited into a relationship so intimate that we might consider it a holy love affair. In this abiding, we begin a transformation that is for the most part indescribable. We are at a loss for words as to how we experience God's presence, but we know that this intimate love affair gives rise to praise and rejoicing, glory and exultation, and comfort and peace.

This blessedness brings us assurance and strength in knowing that God is an ever-present refuge in our time of need. God becomes our focus above all things. God becomes our all in all. We know that there is nothing sweeter, stronger, higher, or wider than the love of God for us, and for us, there is nothing more pleasant or more satisfying in heaven or on earth than our love for our God. When our love for God reaches this height, we understand that divine love knows no limits and overflows all bounds. In receiving this divine love, we should feel no burdens, think nothing of troubles, face all challenges, endure all sufferings, and be free from all doubt because we truly believe all things are possible with God.

Dear disciple, let us experience the great power and assurance found in the divine love affair with our God, for it transforms us into acceptable vessels for God's truth. We hear and know the voice of God, which brings clarity in how to live in our uncertain world by allowing God to change us into bearers of the image of our Savior Jesus for the benefit of others. Divine love is swift, sincere, kind, pleasant, and delightful. Divine love is strong, patient, faithful, prudent, long-suffering, and never self-seeking. Divine love is humble, upright, sober, chaste, firm at times, but always forgiving. Let us taste this sweet love of God and never let it go even in desperate times. Let us embrace our Beloved and receive the assurance of eternal life.

Loving Truly

Jesus said to him, "'You shall love the Lord your God with all your heart, with all your soul, and with all your mind.' This is the first and great commandment. And the second is like it: 'You shall love your neighbor as yourself.' On these two commandments hang all the Law and the Prophets."

—MATTHEW 22:37–40 (NKJV)

As disciples of our Lord Jesus, we need to frequently ask, "Am I a courageous and wise lover?" Without God's presence, we are easily deceived and blinded to our selfish and callous nature. Jesus calls us to love, even as He has loved us, which requires us to love those who are not so lovable. This is a hard task for we must admit that our focus is so often upon our own needs during life's difficulties. We are often quick to give up on the difficult since we are too busy asking, "Where is my consolation?" Scripture tells us clearly that we need God's strength to love generously. We must hear God tell us that even in life's difficulties, we are called to be courageous lovers who stand firm against the temptation to give up on those who require extra grace. We become wise lovers only when we allow God to possess us through the power of the Holy Spirit. Only then can we rebuke the enemy's crafty persuasions and love as Jesus loves. The ability to love is God's greatest gift and is only used wisely when our minds become one with Jesus.

We should know that human emotions are fickle, which causes our love affair with God to wax and wane. Our unstable feelings make us vulnerable to the enemy's attacks as evil thoughts and unhealthy fantasies intrude on our thinking. This should not surprise us for the more closely we bear the image of Jesus, the more despised we become in the eyes of the enemy. The unbelieving world can offer us no help in this task for it cannot and will not understand the ways of Jesus. Our only hope is found in the divine love affair with our Triune God who loves us more than we can imagine.

Dear disciple, let us frequently examine our way of loving before God, knowing that we are weak and lazy lovers. Even in our failure, let us be assured that we are still loved and welcomed unconditionally to unashamedly seek God's forgiveness, wisdom, and strength for the journey. Let us acknowledge the reality of the enemy's attacks and pray daily for protection. Let us shout, "Away unclean spirit! Be gone, wretched seducer! You shall have no part in me, for my Beloved Jesus is my strength! I will not consent to your presence!" Let us arm ourselves with the love of God and say, "The Lord is my light and my salvation. Whom shall I fear?" (Psalm 27:1 NIV). The divine love affair will equip us with an amazing capacity to love. Even as our emotional state waxes and wanes, let us cling to our God and rest assured that in all things, we are more than conquerors because of the ever-present power of God's love.

Seeing Grace through Humility

Do you think the Scriptures have no meaning? They say that God is passionate that the spirit he has placed within us should be faithful to him. And he gives grace generously. As the Scriptures say, "God opposes the proud but gives grace to the humble." So humble yourselves before God. Resist the devil, and he will flee from you. Come close to God, and God will come close to you. Wash your hands, you sinners; purify your hearts, for your loyalty is divided between God and the world. Let there be tears for what you have done. Let there be sorrow and deep grief. Let there be sadness instead of laughter, and gloom instead of joy. Humble yourselves before the Lord, and he will lift you up in honor.

—JAMES 4:5–10 (NLT)

As disciples of our Lord Jesus, we must come to grasp the meaning of humility in order to fully experience the grace of God. The grace of God is a mysterious thing and is described in many ways, but we who have taken on the attitude of humility see the grace of God as a magnanimous gift that gives life and salvation to the unworthy. Blessed are we who learn to wear the mantle of humility. We know God's grace for our loving faith community has demonstrated gracious acts to us and encouraged us toward the humble path. We come to understand humility as an act of surrender by giving up all rights to our selfish ways so that we can turn to God in submissive prayer and ask for divine wisdom concerning all things. In doing this, we experience more fully the love, forgiveness, mercy, and compassion of God and more readily receive godly wisdom while studying God's Word, especially when done in community. When we kneel at the foot of the cross, stare up at Jesus, and receive revelation as to how much God loves us, we will finally begin to understand why the apostle John wrote, "God so loved the world …" (John 3:16 NIV). It is by humility that we willingly examine ourselves according to Jesus's standard and marvel at what God has done to ensure our salvation.

God has made Jesus's way clear to us, and that way is the path of humility. When life is difficult, we must engage more vigorously in our spiritual disciplines; otherwise, our minds will be led astray. So many would be followers of Jesus become impatient and lazy when things go badly. In their weakness, they return to their old worldly ways of poor judgment. The vision of God's grace becomes blurry, and pride, envy, anxiety, and worry take its place. We must understand how vulnerable we are to the enemy's deception, which derails us from the humble path. We must admit our weakness and never think we can successfully tread the path of humility alone! We must be vigilant and impress this truth on those just beginning their journey with Jesus for they are especially vulnerable and must be guarded and guided by those more established in God's truth. We must recognize that there is much Holy Spirit power for transformation when we gather in Jesus's name and willingly submit ourselves to His wisdom for the journey.

Dear disciple, let us always remember that God's presence is very near even in times of distress. Let us recognize that trials and temptations are always opportunities to seek God's instruction, so let us be ready to turn quickly to our God for guidance and strength. Let us be assured that our Savior's consolation will come and will come more quickly as we learn to master the way of humility.

Understanding Our Position before God

In the sweat of your face you shall eat bread Till you return to the ground, For out of it you were taken; For dust you are, And to dust you shall return.

—GENESIS 3:19 (NKJV)

As disciples of our Lord Jesus, humility demands that we know who we are before our Creator God, and this understanding comes only by daily prayer, meditation, and scripture reading. Scripture teaches that our complex being is in reality only dust, which God has fashioned and given the breath of life. This revelation should bring a profound change in the way we think of ourselves and in the way we see our God. As we come to see the amazingly generous gift Jesus has given us, our self-esteem should begin to fade. When the magnitude of the gracious gift of God begins to fill us with divine light, our blindness is removed, and divine truth bears witness to our selfish, sinful lives. Divine revelation can make us feel unclean and worthless. Left unchecked, our faulty human reasoning can cause us to sink into a pit of hopelessness unless we allow the grace of God to rescue us. Thankfully, our Heavenly Father, our Lord Jesus, and the Holy Spirit draws us near and reveals that we have been found worthy to receive God's gracious gifts of love, forgiveness, and eternal life despite our sorry state.

This "good news" should fill us with joy and cause us to run to our God's caring and consoling arms even as we wrestle with the truth of our weakness. What comfort we receive when we look into the face of our Savior Jesus and feel the strength of His compassionate gaze as we resolve to follow the path of righteousness. What a marvelous wonder it is to be rescued from the pit of despair in which we sinners so often find ourselves. It is God's love that graciously supports us through and guards us from so many grave dangers and evils. By coming to our God in faith, we begin to experience the reality and character of our God and also start to see our true selves. It is only by this humbling experience that we enter a true love relationship with our God by which the Holy Spirit can further expand our understanding of the profound truths of life. Any hesitation or fear we may have had in coming to God will melt away as we start to appreciate the bounteous gifts of love and wisdom our God desires to give us.

Dear disciple, let us move past our feelings of unworthiness and enter the blessed relationship with our God, knowing that a never-ending source of faithful love and gracious mercy awaits us. Let us understand that our God loves even those who at present are ungrateful and remain stiff-necked toward the ways of Jesus. Let us pray that they too might come to their senses, repent, and accept Jesus's gracious offer. Let us pray continuously for God's presence and strength to endure the transformation necessary for faithful community service. With thankful, humble, and devout hearts, let us proclaim to all that God is our salvation, our courage, our strength, our wisdom, and our peace and that the "good news" invitation of Jesus is open to all.

Finalizing Our Decisions with God's Help

And now, Israel, what does the Lord your God require of you, but to fear the Lord your God, to walk in all His ways and to love Him, to serve the Lord your God with all your heart and with all your soul, and to keep the commandments of the Lord and His statutes which I command you today for your good.

—DEUTERONOMY 10:12–13 (NKJV)

As disciples of our Lord Jesus, in submission, we must learn to finalize all our decisions before God in order to lead a pleasing and righteous life. In this act, we bear witness that we have truly entered an abiding relationship with our God and completely trust God's wisdom in guiding our every move. We must understand that we are perversely motivated by selfish desires and fears and need the constant presence of God to purify our thinking. Have we not had enough of choosing poorly? Have not our so-called "best laid plans" from our well-ordered lives proved inadequate to rescue us from the uncertainties of life? We need an unchanging source of truth to guide our every decision, and for the follower of Jesus, that source is our Creator God. The closer our relationship moves toward abiding with God, the more abundantly God's grace washes over us. Through God's presence, we experience the highest wisdom flowing like living water, which floods us with blessed grace to guide our every step. Our blessed love affair with God opens our eyes to see our desperate need for Jesus, knowing He is our salvation and our source of true joy. Although we receive physical and material gifts from God, we must understand that true blessedness comes by experiencing God's abiding and loving presence.

We must not be like those who choose to give glory to people or to things rather than to God. If we choose to continue to delight in our own glory, we should expect the reward of a withered and selfish heart possessed by burdens and distress. We must hear Jesus say, "Apart from Me, you can do nothing" (John 15:5 NIV). We must turn to our God and receive grace upon grace so that we are strengthened to "circumcise our hearts" and turn from our stiff-necked ways.

Dear disciple, let us give God all thanks and praise and revel in the glorious presence of the Holy Spirit. Let us embrace our God and receive a new heart that knows nothing of envy, arrogance, prejudice, or selfishness. Let us understand that without God's presence, our human condition influences all our choices and decisions to our detriment. So with grateful hearts, let us rejoice in our God above all things, for no one is good except God, who is to be sought above any worldly wisdom for our every decision.

Sweetness in Serving God

I will sing to the Lord as long as I live; I will sing praise to my God while I have my being. May my meditation be sweet to Him; I will be glad in the Lord.

—PSALM 104:33–34 (NKJV)

Therefore be imitators of God as dear children. And walk in love, as Christ also has loved us and given Himself for us, an offering and a sacrifice to God for a sweet-smelling aroma.

—EPHESIANS 5:1–2 (NKJV)

As disciples of our Lord Jesus, have we discovered the sweetness found in serving our God? This profound state of abiding blessedness found only in the presence of our God is both enjoyed and given as we share Jesus with a broken world. Scripture describes our pleasing service to and for our God as a sweet-smelling aroma that blesses not only us but our God and His kingdom here on earth as well. Our journey toward sweet blessedness begins in prayer as we ask for guidance in attaining the path for service. At first, our conversations with God are cluttered with the asking for many things unrelated to service in the kingdom of God. God gladly hears our prayers but eventually shows us that most of these many things are not necessary and may in fact be unhelpful in achieving our goal. As intimacy with God grows, our attention gradually turns from asking to listening more closely for God's wisdom and guidance. Our prayers and meditations move from selfish wants to godly desires as we develop a heart for God. Our prayers include more thanksgiving and praise to our God and King for His abundant and generous love and mercies. Our cherished time with our Beloved takes on sweetness as we plunge into the fountain of Jesus's unceasing love. We see the dawn of an unwavering hope within us knowing that our God is a God of faithful promises. We revel in the presence of the Holy Spirit and see that all things, gift or discipline, come from God for our benefit. Thus blossom sweet peace and contentment as we enter the high privilege of enjoying all things to God's glory.

Even as many of God's ways remain a mystery, we should never stop pursuing all that our generous God would reveal to us. Receiving the sweetness of divine revelation is attained only by a most intimate relationship with the Father, the Son, and the Holy Spirit and can at times be overwhelming. By condescending to our low estate, our Lord Jesus has shown us the way, the truth, and the life by which we may live in blessedness with our Creator. We must, therefore, allow our minds to be transformed in order to receive godly eyes that see the great honor and glory involved in serving our God. We begin this path as servants in the kingdom of God, but as our love affair grows, God reveals to us a more precious status for we are, in fact, God's children upon whom our Creator God bestows an eternal inheritance. Is this not *good news?*

Dear disciple, let us join together in singing sweet songs of praise as we enter joyful service to the One who makes us truly free and holy. Let us allow ourselves to be bound to our God by the Holy Spirit in blessedness so that we might become a blessing to others. Let us cling tightly to our Lord and Savior and revel in God's great gift of grace so that we might be empowered to release our tight grasp on worldly things and offer ourselves as living sacrifices to God's glory—a sweet aroma to be enjoyed by all.

STILL LACKING WISDOM

The fear of the Lord is the beginning of wisdom, And the knowledge of the Holy One is understanding.

—PROVERBS 9:10 (NKJV)

As disciples of our Lord Jesus, we should be ever listening for the whisperings of God telling us that we still lack wisdom and are failing to rely on the Holy Spirit for guidance. Our pride is an ever-present obstacle to hearing Jesus's words "you of little faith" (Matthew 14:31 NIV), so let us admit that the longings of our hearts are often far from the will of our God. It is God's desire that we conform our longings entirely to the divine covenant of love and cease our selfish ways. Without God, we are inflamed by our fleshy desires to pursue destructive paths without considering the consequences, so before we act, we should pause and consider whether our doing is for God's honor or for our selfish gain. Let us stop cherishing our darling lusts and be freed from our heavy burdens that cause a troubled conscience. If doing God's will is the motivation behind all of our actions, we will be content with whatever God ordains.

If we truly want to be followers of Jesus, we must forsake our own will and not be driven by unchecked desires, which at best lead us to brief pleasure. We have experienced and should, therefore, recognize the path that leads to a guilty conscience that requires us to beg forgiveness from our God over and over again. How many times must we be reminded that Jesus has shown us the way, the truth, and the life we so desperately desire? Do we not yet understand that we must devote ourselves to God in prayer and wholeheartedly seek God's divine guidance and strength? God has given us many good things to enjoy, but our greatest enjoyment is found in God alone. In fact, we do not know how to enjoy God's gifts properly without first enjoying God, the very source of joy. We must be filled with divine wisdom through a life disciplined by God in order to enter a holy fortress of protection that can guard our distracted minds and unrestrained hearts.

Dear disciple, let us recognize our fragile human condition and seek our God with all our heart, soul, mind, and strength. Let us recognize our need for God's chastisement so that we might turn from our wicked ways and receive God's wisdom. Let us subject ourselves to God's holy commandments and teachings so that we see our sin and our need for a Savior. Let us stop succumbing to our sensual appetites, which creates scandal for ourselves and brings shame to our God. Let us give up the title of hypocrite, and let God be our all in all so that we will be satisfied with and take pleasure in our lives in all circumstances.

Patience to Overcome

Therefore, as God's chosen people, holy and dearly loved, clothe yourselves with compassion, kindness, humility, gentleness and patience. Bear with each other and forgive one another if any of you has a grievance against someone. Forgive as the Lord forgave you. And over all these virtues put on love, which binds them all together in perfect unity. Let the peace of Christ rule in your hearts, since as members of one body you were called to peace. And be thankful.

—COLOSSIANS 3:12–15 (NIV)

As disciples of our Lord Jesus, we must come to realize our complete need for God's help in dealing with the many adversities encountered in this life. Try as we may, we cannot develop any plan that will shield our lives from pain and sorrow. We are often told to approach God in prayer and ask for patience to endure our times of trial and tribulation, but do we actually understand our prayer request? The patience we ask for is not some God-given superpower that makes us immune to our troubles. Patience hinges on our relationship with God and our faith community. Patience is resting in God's presence and trusting in the Holy Spirit's guidance. Patience is relying on godly friends who love and support us in our time of need. God does not intend for us to be free of temptation or opposition in this life. God's desire for us is to find peace by abiding in the love of Jesus by the Holy Spirit and the body of Christ, our faith community, while we are tormented with tribulations and adversities.

The world tries to give us the illusion that wealth and fame are the key to a life of ease that is free from suffering, but as followers of Jesus, are we still so clueless to think that more money or possessions will give us peace? Those with great worldly wealth do seem to have whatever they wish, but closer examination reveals otherwise. Trusting in worldly treasures and pleasures brings nothing but bitterness, weariness, and fear. Worldly blind reasoning leads to a vain pursuit of peace, and instead of finding joy, the result is shame and sorrow. How brief, how false, and how unfulfilling are the results of this journey! Those who long for this wretched path travel through life in a fog while corrupting their souls for the miserly enjoyment of vanity.

Dear disciple, let us understand that the patience we seek to endure our trials and temptations is found only in the abiding presence of God. Let us hear the psalmist say, "Delight yourself in the LORD; and He will give you the desires of your heart" (Psalm 37:4 NKJV). If we wish to be truly delighted and more abundantly comforted, we must spend time with God in prayer, meditation, and scripture reading and be devoted to communion with faithful followers of our Savior Jesus. We must shun worldly solace and find a sweeter, stronger comfort in our God. Let us understand that habits already formed will resist our efforts and cause us sadness and confusion, but perseverance in spiritual disciplines will ultimately reward us with victory in overcoming our sinful ways. Let us embrace God's presence, which quenches our fleshy desires and fills us with the overcoming power of the Holy Spirit. This is the only path that allows us to slam the door in the face of our former ways.

Counting the Cost

And if you do not carry your own cross and follow me, you cannot be my disciple. "But don't begin until you count the cost. For who would begin construction of a building without first calculating the cost to see if there is enough money to finish it?"

—LUKE 14:27–28 (NLT)

Don't trap yourself by making a rash promise to God and only later counting the cost.

—PROVERBS 20:25 (NLT)

As disciples of our Lord Jesus, we may readily admit that our Savior's life is to be our guide in all matters, but are we taken aback when we hear Jesus say, "Have you counted the cost?" (Luke 14:28 NLT). This challenging statement is troubling for us because when we think about the "cost" of following Jesus, we conjure up images of losing the things we value. We begin to ask ourselves questions, such as "Can I afford this?" "What do I have to give up for this?" "Will there be pain or suffering involved?" or "Is the cost really worth the gain?" Allowing these thoughts to consume our minds causes us to freeze in our path of discipleship for which Jesus has called us, unless we can see past the cost to the great treasure Jesus is offering. We must be willing to bear our cross of obedience and humility in order to move toward our goal. Our minds must be possessed by the Holy Spirit to succeed in overcoming our fleshy desires; otherwise, the path toward Christian perfection will remain an oil-covered mountain.

As followers of Jesus, we must quickly learn to submit ourselves to our Lord and Savior in order to conquer our sinful ways. The enemy will continue to pour oil on our path unless our selfish inner desires are overcome by the gracious gift of God's presence and guidance. We must confess that we are our worst enemy and often struggle with a troubled conscience that wrestles between our darling lusts and our desire to follow Jesus. We must look in the mirror daily, see the truth, and then fall to our knees and cry out, "Help me, Lord Jesus! Help me to be humble! Help me to be obedient!"

Dear disciple, it takes the abiding presence of God for us to "love our neighbor as ourselves," but if we love ourselves too much, we will not submit ourselves to the needs of others. We are only dust without God's breath of life, so why is it so hard for us to subject ourselves to others for the sake of God? Did not our Creator God subject Himself to the lowest state for us? Did Jesus not become the most humble and lowest of all men so that we might receive God's gracious power to overcome our sinful self? Let us hear God's truth, learn humility, and obey our Creator! Let us abide in Jesus and allow Him to break our stubborn will. Let us become zealous against our prideful, arrogant self and receive Holy Spirit power so that we are enabled to pay the disciple's cost. Let us subject ourselves to God's transforming power and become empowered to reflect Jesus to everyone we encounter.

Insidious Pride

Pride goes before destruction, And a haughty spirit before a fall.

—PROVERBS 16:18 (NKJV)

Pride ends in humiliation, while humility brings honor.

—PROVERBS 29:23 (NLT)

As disciples of our Lord Jesus, we should never rest on our past achievements but bravely and earnestly ask ourselves if we are still guilty of pride. Our pridefulness is so ingrained that as we read scripture, we may be tempted to gloss over the many judgments proclaimed against the proud. We should appreciate the "fear and trembling" displayed by the faithful who suddenly find themselves face-to-face with God and truly realize their sinful state. We should see the vanity in thinking that we have a right to claim merit for ourselves because of our good deeds. We should hear scripture tell us that even angelic beings, though created for a good purpose, suffer judgment for going against God's wishes. We must come to grips with our blindness if we presume to believe we deserve accolades and praise for doing God's will.

As followers of Jesus, we must remember that without God,

there is no holiness, there is no wisdom, there is no guidance, there is no strength to persevere, there is no virtue, there is no true love, and there is no forgiveness. We must constantly ask God to be our strength in overcoming our pride. Left to ourselves, we fall into the slimy pit of self-indulgence and perish unless we come to our senses and grasp God's gracious hand, which lifts us up to life. We are so prone to being tossed by the waves of opinion and flattery that we forget how truly unstable our thinking is without God's presence. We must remember that this "good news" is the truth that sets us free to become that for which God created us.

Dear disciple, let us pray for God to inflame our lukewarm hearts and lead us to obedience and humility. Let us give God all thanks and praise and in the presence of the Holy Spirit remember that we are but dust transformed into living flesh, talking clay that our Creator has molded. In arrogance, shall we claim God's glory for ourselves? How can we, whose hearts are truly subject to the will of God and who are allowed to call God "Father," dare to even consider such vanity? Does not our blessed Lord Jesus tell us of the folly of gaining the whole world at the cost of our souls (Matthew 16:26 NLT)? Let us forever be committed to praying without ceasing so that we never leave God's presence. Let us understand that unless the abiding presence of God is our fortress, we will forever remain under the power of our cherished misconceptions that lead us to very unhappy endings.

That Which Is Desirable

Finally, brothers and sisters, whatever is true, whatever is noble, whatever is right, whatever is pure, whatever is lovely, whatever is admirable—if anything is excellent or praiseworthy—think about such things. Whatever you have learned or received or heard from me, or seen in me—put it into practice. And the God of peace will be with you.

—PHILIPPIANS 4:8–9 (NIV)

As disciples of our Lord Jesus, we should constantly ask for God's guidance concerning the desirable things in life. Each and every day, we are given opportunities to make choices concerning the events of life, and our actions, however big or small, are guided by what we consider most beneficial. Our choices tend to be rather selfish until we have received guidance from our faith community and begin spending serious time with God asking for discernment. At this point, we should hear Jesus ask if our choices and actions are bringing honor and glory to His name. In our time of meditation, we should examine our actions to see if they are pleasing to God and beneficial to the welfare of our soul. If the answer is yes, then many blessings are shared. If the answer is no, we should pray fervently for God to remove any evil desire from our heart. We should remember that not every desire we experience is Holy Spirit approved, even though that desire seemed acceptable in our past. This divinely revealed wisdom should be a warning for us to *not* rely on our own judgment; otherwise, we risk being deceived into actions that result in consequences affecting not only us but also those whom we love.

As followers of Jesus, we must admit our weakness and not let our pride and arrogance deceive us. We must place every desire before God and in humility receive counsel from the Holy Spirit. We must commit the whole matter to our Creator and with true resignation say, "LORD God, You know what is best for me, so let Your will be done as You please, for Your honor and glory." By abiding in our God, we are strengthened in divine wisdom, which results in assurance in knowing the desirable things of life. We should feel the consolation of God in the matter of decisions and experience excitement in achieving victory over self all because we placed ourselves in God's hands and allowed the Holy Spirit to deal freely with us in all things. God's consolation comes when we realize that our truest and best desire is to obey and live a pleasing life before our Creator.

Dear disciple, let us admit that we require much grace and mercy from our God in order to choose the desirable things in life, for we are prideful, selfish, and weak. Let us pray continually for Holy Spirit power to work discernment within us every moment of every day. Let us pray that our desires and our will align perfectly with the will of God, which is always pleasing and acceptable. Let us commit to scripture study in fellowship so that we become infused with divine wisdom. As children of God, let us become one with God so that we are no longer able to choose our own way. Let us take for ourselves the heart and mind of Jesus so that we no longer struggle with inappropriate desires. Let us wholeheartedly follow the path of our Savior so that we may find rest, peace, and freedom in choosing amid the difficult and troubling things of life.

WHERE DO I FIND COMFORT?

Praise be to the God and Father of our Lord Jesus Christ, the Father of compassion and the God of all comfort, who comforts us in all our troubles, so that we can comfort those in any trouble with the comfort we ourselves receive from God. For just as we share abundantly in the sufferings of Christ, so also our comfort abounds through Christ.

—2 CORINTHIANS 1:3–5 (NIV)

As disciples of our Lord Jesus, we should examine ourselves before God asking, "Where do I truly seek comfort?" for we are often guilty of choosing our truth over God's truth. We may say that God is our source of comfort, but our lives often prove us to be hypocrites. Our delusions run so deep that unless we intentionally spend time in prayer, meditation, and scripture reading, we will remain ill equipped to understand why God is to be our sole source of comfort. Surrounding ourselves with faithful followers of Jesus is essential, for we need direction and encouragement in this truth. It is a hard task for us to understand the reality that worldly comforts are temporary at best, but once we see the vanity of worldly solutions, we should strive wholeheartedly to gain assurance that comfort, peace, and joy are found in God alone.

The world would convince us that the possession of created things or the pursuit of illicit relationships brings us the joy and comfort we so desperately want, but Jesus teaches us that comfort and joy are found only in the heavenly promises of our God. God has created many good things for us to enjoy, but when we cling too tightly to these present things, we lose sight of God's blessed love, mercy, and forgiveness that bring us true comfort. We should, therefore, pursue the blessings of God through the abiding presence of the Holy Spirit and abandon our false hope of finding comfort in the things of this world. Only in the presence of God will we find true consolation, for it is in prayer and the company of our Christian brothers and sisters that our fears are dispelled and the reality of being loved is assured.

Dear disciple, let us stay vigilant when assaulted by the things of this world that bring anxiety, worry, and fear. In our desire for comfort, let us shun the vain and brief solutions of the world and turn to our God. Let us cry out to our Savior, "Be with me, Lord Jesus, in everything I say and do," and let the truth of Jesus be our comfort and our guide. Let us turn from human folly and ask God to help us understand the depth of the love of Jesus and the assurance of God's eternal promise to never leave or forsake us. Let us proclaim that the truth of God will be our satisfaction no matter our circumstances. Let us become devoted to our God and experience living water to sooth our troubled souls.

Do We Allow God to Care for Us?

Humble yourselves, therefore, under God's mighty hand, that he may lift you up in due time. Cast all your anxiety on him because he cares for you.

—1 PETER 5:6–7 (NIV)

As disciples of our Lord Jesus, are we allowing ourselves to be used by God solely for God's purpose? In order to answer this question, we must honestly decide if we fully trust God's help in making all of our decisions. Our first move is to admit that our decision-making ability is often distorted by our sensual desires. Jesus has taught us that enticing temptations are ever present and that we need Holy Spirit guidance to know what is best for us. If we allow God to help us mature in these understandings, we will admit to our need for God's care in order to avoid making poor decisions. We need to develop the habit of casting all our cares upon Jesus; otherwise, we place ourselves on a precarious path. Unless we allow Jesus to wipe the scales from our eyes, we will remain blinded by the world's many shiny solutions and will never see the glorious path of righteousness as our only option for goodness. Since we can see no farther than our next step, our minds are prone to conjuring many worries and anxieties about the unknown. Devotion to the path of Jesus is our only hope in overcoming our blindness to the goodness of casting our cares upon our Savior.

In casting our cares upon Jesus, we are asking God to comfort us with love and guide us with divine wisdom toward the solutions we need in life. We also must see the necessity of God's discipline in caring for us because our undisciplined ways cause such a mess. Understanding God's ways of truth concerning our care should lead us to praise God in our times of affliction and darkness as well as in our times of comfort and delight for we now should realize that the presence of God is our joy in all things. Casting our cares upon God builds up our trust and faith in God's mysterious ways for us and entices us to draw even closer. We hear Jesus call to us, "If you wish to walk with Me, be as ready to suffer as to enjoy; be as willingly to be destitute and poor as to be rich and satisfied" (Matthew 5:11–13 NIV).

Dear disciple, let us say to our Lord and Savior that we shall live to bring glory to His name. Let us give up trying to care for ourselves apart from God and learn to depend on Holy Spirit guidance for all our cares. Let us be grateful in all things, knowing that God's hand is upon us through times good and evil, sweet and bitter, and joyful and sorrowful. Let us hear Jesus clearly say, "Do not fear, for I am with you!" Let us cast ourselves into the abiding and caring presence of God the Father, God the Son, and God, the Holy Spirit so that all our fears and anxieties are replaced with the joy-filled life that satisfies our every desire.

Suffering

Remember your word to your servant, for you have given me hope. My comfort in my suffering is this: Your promise preserves my life.

—PSALM 119:49–50 (NIV)

Now if we are children, then we are heirs—heirs of God and co-heirs with Christ, if indeed we share in his sufferings in order that we may also share in his glory. I consider that our present sufferings are not worth comparing with the glory that will be revealed in us.

—ROMANS 8:17–18 (NIV)

As disciples of our Lord Jesus, how are we to understand and respond to suffering? There are many messages found in scripture that address suffering, but have we heard them? There is much suffering in the world that seems unfair, undeserved, and discriminatory, and we are at a loss to explain why it must exist, but as for our own suffering, we should look to Jesus for our response. Jesus came from heaven out of love for His creation to suffer greatly for our salvation. He bore patiently false accusations and disgrace without complaint. For His blessings, he received ingratitude, for His miracles, blasphemies, and for His teachings, scorn. Jesus tells us clearly that if we choose to be His disciples, we should be ready to receive the same treatment. Thanks be to God that Jesus's message doesn't end here!

No one wants to endure suffering, so what should be our response to this? Should we not admit the reality of suffering in our broken world and seek understanding, encouragement, and comfort from our God and our faith community? As disciples, we should hear Jesus's teachings and see that His exemplary life is our guide in response to our suffering. We must grow to know that we are not alone in our suffering. We are called to abide in our God and receive Holy Spirit power to live patiently according to God's will. We should see that suffering is a result of the world's sinful condition and that we, miserable sinners that we are, are called to bear the burden of our sinful human condition even as we allow God to redeem us for eternal life. It is by the transforming, gracious touch of God that we can rest assured in our suffering and even say that life is bright and full of beauty. We should now see the depth of God's grace, for Jesus has opened for us the kingdom of heaven, both now and forevermore, by His death, resurrection, and ascension into heaven. The reality of God's presence in our lives through our faith community should help us overcome any suffering.

Dear disciple, should we not give all thanks and praise for God's presence in our suffering, for we have been ransomed by Jesus and now stand innocent before our God? As one of God's elect, we should proclaim that we have been found worthy to suffer for our God. Let us commit ourselves to the ways of Jesus and be forever strengthened by the presence of the Holy Spirit, which is most profoundly experienced in our faith community. Let us pray for the many who remain trapped in their suffering so that their eyes might be opened to godly truth, and let us pray for ourselves that we never return to a lukewarm faith that cannot lead us to the joy-filled life even as we suffer.

Patience in Suffering

But what can I say? He has spoken to me, and he himself has done this. I will walk humbly all my years because of this anguish of my soul. Lord, by such things people live; and my spirit finds life in them too. You restored me to health and let me live. Surely it was for my benefit that I suffered such anguish. In your love you kept me from the pit of destruction; you have put all my sins behind your back.

—ISAIAH 38:15–17 (NIV)

As disciples of our Lord Jesus, have we clearly heard scripture's message from both Jesus and His apostles concerning our suffering? Our usual response to suffering is to moan and complain and ask, "Why me?" but the saints of old join with the voices from scripture to proclaim unanimously that suffering must come to the faithful followers of Jesus. It takes much time with God, scripture, and the faith community for us to understand the necessity of suffering. If our response to suffering is anger or impatience, we cannot hear the voice of Jesus calling us to a deeper understanding of His ways. We set up our pity party, a table for one—me, myself, and I—and dwell on our sorry state rather than asking God to help us understand. Are we afraid to let Jesus show us just how childish we are? Can we bear to hear Him say, "Take a look around and compare your suffering to others."

If we are willing to receive the wisdom of God, we will hear Him say, "I am allowing this suffering for your own good. I am trying to draw you near so that you can learn more fully your dependence on Me." We must ask God for patience in this journey. One of the great teachings from God is that true patience is only found when we become totally dependent on God. The apostle Paul heard this message clearly and proclaims that God's power is made perfect in us when we realize our weakness (2 Corinthians 12:9 NIV). It is God's power through the Holy Spirit that makes us strong, but we are so prideful and stubborn that it often takes suffering for us to realize our weakness and our need for God's help. Our reward-oriented "What's in it for me?" thinking can prevent us from understanding that our greatest reward is found in an intimate knowing of our Father God, our Lord Jesus, and the Holy Spirit. This transformed way of thinking results in profound revelation, understanding, and newness of life.

Dear disciple, let us pray for God's grace to empower us in overcoming our blind and corrupt way of thinking. Let us recognize that suffering, which may torment and discourages us for a time, is a call to come to our senses and run to the arms of Jesus, who is our wisdom, comfort, and strength. Let us ask our God to reveal the depth of His love for us and the necessity of suffering as discipline so that we might become true bearers of Jesus's image to the world.

Confessing Our Weakness

But he said to me, "My grace is sufficient for you, for power is made perfect in weakness." So, I will boast all the more gladly of my weaknesses, so that the power of Christ may dwell in me. Therefore I am content with weaknesses, insults, hardships, persecutions, and calamities for the sake of Christ; for whenever I am weak, then I am strong.

—2 CORINTHIANS 12:9–10 (NRSV)

As disciples of our Lord Jesus, have we come to grips with how dependent we are on God's provision? Has it become our practice to confess our weakness to Jesus every moment of every day? Shouldn't we examine our lives continually and face the fact that we often succumb to the smallest temptations? Without Holy Spirit guidance, the slightest trifle can lead us to indulging in the most grievous temptations. We often delude ourselves by believing we have mastered our desires until we experience an unexpected attack that causes us to revert to old sinful ways. This should prove to us that we are weak and at risk from the slightest breeze. We must look to our Lord Jesus, admit our frail state of mind, and say, "Have mercy on me a sinner; pull me out of my slimy pit of despair and place me on Your righteous path." Our weakness in resisting our passions shows that we are fools to think we can escape this state of corruption without God's help. As long as we persist in our "do it myself" fantasy, our unbridled passions will continue to assault us with grief and bitterness. We must wake up to this reality or forever suffer the consequences.

Our victory in overcoming our weakness is found by asking God almighty for wisdom and strength in this undertaking. It is only by God's presence that we are enabled to turn our fleshy desires toward heavenly treasures. We must pray for transformation of our confused minds and let go of the delusion that our envious and lustful hearts can be satisfied by the delights of this broken world. Is it not insanity to know the world as being false and vain yet refuse to give it up? If we continue down this path of destruction, does this not prove the power our misguided desires have over us?

Dear disciple, let us admit that without God, we are blind to the consequences of pursuing worldly pleasures, thinking there are delights beneath the thorns. Let us taste the sweetness of God and break away from this wickedness. Let us receive the wisdom of God found only in holy discipline so that we can renounce our worldly ways. Let us cry out to our Savior and pray, "Lord Jesus, help me overcome my delusions and ignorance. Help me see how greatly the world has deceived me. Help me find satisfaction in Your presence and in the fellowship with Your faithful followers. Increase my faith so that I might enter Your eternal peace."

Do We Appreciate God's Gifts?

Each of you should use whatever gift you have received to serve others, as faithful stewards of God's grace in its various forms. If anyone speaks, they should do so as one who speaks the very words of God. If anyone serves, they should do so with the strength God provides, so that in all things God may be praised through Jesus Christ. To him be the glory and the power for ever and ever. Amen.

—1 PETER 4:10–11 (NIV)

As disciples of our Lord Jesus, do we truly appreciate the gifts of God? We may say that God has given us many good things to enjoy and that God provides for our every need, but is this only lip service? We may say we believe and trust in the grace of God, but our lives often betray us as hypocrites. We are guilty of saying many flattering things about God, but the focus of our lives is more often on ourselves as we misuse God's gracious gifts. When our shameful behavior is revealed to us, we should admit that God's truth is not yet within us, which should cause us to seek God's forgiveness and ask for revelation concerning God's gift of grace. The good news of Jesus reminds us that we are no longer slaves to our sorry state for hope is found in prayer, study, and Christian community, which gives us the means for God's wisdom to sink in. When we wholeheartedly seek and invite God to overwhelm us with the presence of the Holy Spirit, we see a stark reality. God must be our all in all, and we must rest in God alone in order for us to see the magnitude of God's grace. The mighty work our God has accomplished to save us from ourselves for service in the kingdom of God and to eternal life takes a lifetime to appreciate. As we start to appreciate divine grace, our actions should proclaim that God alone is our source of power, sufficiency, satisfaction, consolation, beauty, nobility, perfection, forgiveness, and love. Understanding the gracious call of Jesus should cause us to turn from worshiping the creation to the worship of the Creator!

As lovers of Jesus, we should give all honor and glory to God above health, beauty, honor, power, dignity, cleverness, riches, arts, joy, fame, praise, merit, and desire. We should pray for freedom from such vanities that entangle us and impede our path toward a humble and thankful heart. Let us celebrate the light of God's presence and be liberated from the shackles and chains of sinful thinking. Let us cling to our hope and salvation found only in the Father, the Son, and the Holy Spirit.

Dear disciple, our primary purpose is to know our God for God alone is our wisdom in understanding love. God alone empowers us to love as Jesus loves, which is to love our Triune God fully and love our neighbor completely. God's gracious gifts alone give us glad and generous hearts that empower us to see as Jesus sees and love as Jesus loves. Let us give all thanks and praise to our God who frees us from poor judgment and enables us for kingdom service. Let us truly learn to appreciate God's gifts and give the Holy Spirit permission to recreate us to be God's true image bearers.

Understanding the Gift of God

Jesus answered her, "If you knew the gift of God and who it is that asks you for a drink, you would have asked him and he would have given you living water."

—JOHN 4:10 (NIV)

As disciples of our Lord Jesus, what comes to mind when we hear the term "gift of God"? We might reason that all things come from God and are, therefore, God's gifts, but as we grow in divine understanding, we might choose to be more specific in our description. We can count our many physical gifts with our five senses, such as life, health, talents, family, friends, work, and material possessions, but we should understand the tenuous and temporal nature of these things. More importantly, there are the spiritual or supernatural things associated with God that may be harder to describe but are seen as more precious, for these are things eternal that bring us true life, the promised living water of Jesus. We truly begin to appreciate the difference between the temporal and the eternal once we choose to pursue God with all our heart, soul, mind, and strength. We see Jesus offer the woman at the well the ultimate gift of God: living water that forever satisfies. Many understand this as the promised gift of the Holy Spirit resulting from Jesus's ministry, death, resurrection, and ascension to God the Father. Upon understanding the value of this gift, we should willingly release ourselves into a love affair with our God and be filled with the supernatural gift that brings meaning and purpose to our lives.

The divine love affair should help us accept something we usually do not see as a gift and that is the gift of obedience. We usually see obedience as an act of effort on our part rather than as a gift from God, but by spending time with God and fellow disciples, we come to see that obedience is actually the living out of our transformed lives for the kingdom of God. This is solely the gift of God's grace, not the result of our will. The works we used to do out of guilt or to earn God's favor become acts of devotion that bring us joy and fulfillment. The gift of obedience gives our lives meaning and purpose of the highest order for the benefit of those around us.

Dear disciple, it is so easy for us to be disillusioned by the fact that gifts, both physical and spiritual, are not given equally, especially those of a material nature. We can be possessed by any number of destructive behaviors, such as being envious, bitter, greedy, self-righteousness, judgmental, lustful, superior, gossipy, stingy, or unforgiving, all of which destroy the relationships our God holds dear. We desperately need God and the faith community to hold us accountable so that we use God's gifts wisely, so let us pray without ceasing for the gift of humility. We must have the attitude of Christ Jesus if we are to increasingly receive the gift of God's grace so that we might bring glory to our God in everything we say and do.

Humility, Liberty, and Peace

Those who live according to the flesh have their minds set on what the flesh desires; but those who live in accordance with the Spirit have their minds set on what the Spirit desires. The mind governed by the flesh is death, but the mind governed by the Spirit is life and peace.

—ROMANS 8:5–6 (NIV)

So the last will be first, and the first will be last.

—MATTHEW 20:16 (NIV)

As disciples of our Lord Jesus, we study scripture to clarify our path toward blessed liberty and peace in life but often fail to appreciate the importance of humility for our journey. We are told to focus our desires on God's will, but unless we are willing to surrender completely to God's ways, we cannot be empowered for a life of devotion to God's will. Part of our objection to God's guidance is the command to respect the authority of others who demand obedience to their will. Those with authority over us may or may not be godly, but lessons in obedience are essential for us to understand the path to humility. Without these lessons, we continue to moan and complain about having to do what we are told. How can we expect to attain the liberty and peace found in God without persevering in obedience, for this is the path that allows God to open our eyes to the necessity of humility?

Another aspect concerning the path to liberty and peace is learning the value of having less rather than more. Greed and envy are evil vices that rob us of peace and choke our compassion, thus separating us from both God and neighbor. If we claim to be followers of Jesus, we should be satisfied and grateful for God's provisions and refuse to covet that which we do not have. Are we not yet tired of the consequences of chasing our fleshy desires to satisfy our lusts? We remain shackled in our selfishness unless we allow the abiding presence of God to guide us into a faith community that will teach us humility and show us how to love.

The attitude of humility is essential in obtaining liberty and peace. Being satisfied as the least and last frees us to receive God's blessed peace by stepping aside and allowing others to receive honor and praise. Being humble enables God to fill us with Holy Spirit power, which unshackles us from our self-righteous perspective concerning others and allows us to be satisfied with God alone. Without God, all we can see is injustice as we are passed over or not recognized for our "great contributions." We resort to shameful behavior gossiping about or lashing out at the success of the "less deserving." We must be greatly disciplined by God and held accountable by other devoted disciples before we can attain humility.

Dear disciple, let us appreciate the difficult path we face in obtaining liberty and peace. Let us understand that God's discipline ultimately leads to joy even in the turmoil of life. It is Holy Spirit power that helps us see the truth in Jesus's path of humility. As the light of God replaces the darkness and despair of our old ways, we receive the blessed assurance of a life filled with liberty and peace, all because we allow humility to become our new reality. Let us let God's discipline transform us into worthy vessels to receive the living water of Jesus so that the peace of God liberates us to bless others with love, compassion, and forgiveness.

Our Throne or God's

Then I heard every creature in heaven and on earth and under the earth and on the sea, and all that is in them, saying: "To him who sits on the throne and to the Lamb be praise and honor and glory and power, for ever and ever!" The four living creatures said, "Amen," and the elders fell down and worshiped.

—REVELATION 5:13–14 (NIV)

As disciples of our Lord Jesus, are we brave enough to look in the mirror and tell God, "I am no longer the center of my universe"? Do we have the courage to be honest and admit that it is a very hard task to give up the throne from which we make our judgments? As we begin to allow God's wisdom to sink in, we should take care so that we do not remain the self-righteous judge of others. Making progress in overcoming our sinful ways can be difficult, but overcoming our judgment of others may be the hardest thing to give up. Scripture clearly tells us that judgment belongs to God. Our job is to witness the way, truth, and life of Jesus to others and then let the Holy Spirit do God's work.

Why are we so consumed with gossip concerning the affairs of others? Doesn't this behavior stir up unrest and discontent within us and fuel our judgment of those who to our mind seem clueless? Do we not believe that God knows the mind, heart, and intensions of everyone? Should we not leave their end in God's hands and stop judging them? There is much strife and injustice in the world, so instead of gossiping and complaining about situations we cannot change, shouldn't we witness the kingdom of God as best we can in Christian action and leave judgment to God?

Dear disciple, shouldn't our focus be on disciplining ourselves and not on judging others' failures? If they seek our fellowship, we should be faithful witnesses of Jesus showing compassion, love, and forgiveness. If they fail, we should encourage them. If they leave our fellowship, we should let them go. But if we find ourselves still judging others, let us admit that we are still clinging to the throne that rightly belongs to our God. Let us commit to praying for guidance before we act. Let us never stop looking in the mirror asking, "Is God king of my life, or am I?"

Progress toward Peace

I will listen to what God the Lord says; he promises peace to his people, his faithful servants—but let them not turn to folly. Surely his salvation is near those who fear him, that his glory may dwell in our land. Love and faithfulness meet together; righteousness and peace kiss each other.

—PSALM 85:8–10 (NIV)

As disciples of our Lord Jesus, we should frequently pray and meditate on whether we have made any progress in finding peace. Are our minds still in turmoil even as we hear Jesus say, "Peace I leave with you; My peace I give to you; not as the world gives do I give to you. Do not let your heart be troubled, nor let it be fearful" (John 14:27 NIV). If our minds are not at peace, we must ask if we truly desire the things required to receive the peace Jesus offers. If we are guilty of this deficiency, we must admit that we have not sought the presence of God often enough or sincerely asked for help in overcoming our unbelief concerning that which would bring us peace of mind. If we would only listen to God while in prayer, we would hear Him say, "Will you do what is required to receive My peace?"

A humble heart is required to receive the peace of God, for a humble heart allows God to transform our troubled and doubting minds. Humility makes us worthy vessels for the Holy Spirit, which can then impart a calm spirit that impacts our every thought and action. Our every intention becomes directed toward pleasing God as peacemakers rather than troublemakers. Our new peace of mind should keep us from rashly judging the words and deeds of others and entangling ourselves in affairs that are not our concern. Our minds should no longer dwell on troubling issues but on God as the solution. How can we find peace of mind if we continue in these futile and fruitless activities? Our lives are often full of trouble and uncertainty, but the apostle Paul passes on to us that God's grace is sufficient for all our needs (2 Corinthians 12:9 NIV). God's power is perfected in us when we are truly humble. Our weakness is replaced by God's presence.

Dear disciple, we make progress toward God's peace only by offering ourselves daily to the divine will of God with all our heart. We cannot find peace as long as we cling to our corrupt thinking and selfish ways. We must stop trying to control things that cannot be controlled. We must stop worrying about the future and quit dwelling on the what-ifs. We must stop trying to justify our actions as if human reasoning can sway God. We must acknowledge that God is just in all things divine and deserves all honor and praise. If we truly want the peace of God, which surpasses all our understanding, we must stay true to the righteous path of Jesus and dwell in the presence of the Holy Spirit. It is in this abiding that we enjoy an abundance of peace as much as is possible in this earthly life.

Freedom through Prayer

They devoted themselves to the apostles' teaching and to fellowship, to the breaking of bread and to prayer.

—ACTS 2:42 (NIV)

Devote yourselves to prayer, being watchful and thankful.

—COLOSSIANS 4:2 (NIV)

As disciples of our Lord Jesus, we must understand that it takes more than reading and study to understand God's Word. We must constantly plead, "Help me understand," as we humbly sit before God in prayer and wait in silence for divine revelation concerning what we have studied. The mysterious, transforming power of scripture is given to us only when we allow the Holy Spirit to free our minds from our corrupt preconceived notions. Our minds are so contaminated with worldly influence and human reasoning that we can scarcely hear God speak truth concerning the important things of life. We want "do-it-yourself" instant gratification to life's challenges, which is very different from God's ways of transformation. How many times must we fail in our search for truth before we turn wholeheartedly to God? Is it really that hard for us to understand that God's ways are not ours? We need godly wisdom, and this requires guidance from devout followers of the ways of Jesus. We need to be assisted in our prayer life to receive all that the Holy Spirit would give us so that we fully understand scripture. The Bible cannot transform our thinking unless its words become more than intellectual facts, and this requires prayerful listening. Prayer is designed by God to change us, which requires us to bring a head full of scripture to God with less talking and more listening all the while pleading, "Help me understand." Prayer is not a forum for bargaining with God.

The world has deceived us into thinking that we are entitled to get our way. When we go to God with our worldly requests and get no response, we are often moved to anger or disappointment perhaps even to the point of questioning God's existence. We must allow God to free our minds from worldly expectations so that the Holy Spirit can fill our minds with truth. The cares of this world entangle us, and the necessities of the body ensnare us filling us with anxiety, worry, and fear. It is so hard for us to let go of our worldly ways so that we can receive this truth that God truly loves us and will provide for us. Scripture speaks truth to us about the absolute necessity of being part of a faith community. They are the source of God's love and guidance for us in our time of need. We may pray in private for help in understanding God's truth, but we should share our prayer concerns with the faith community so that they can be God's hands and feet to us.

Dear disciple, if we are ever to be freed to fully serve in God's kingdom, we must surrender to listening and hearing God's call for us to receive the Holy Spirit's transforming wisdom and stop depending solely on our scholarly knowledge and worldly understanding. Let us humbly pray that we receive the Holy Spirit's overcoming power to conquer our selfish, carnal desires. Let us allow God to replace our bitterness and disappointment with blessed comfort and understanding. Our minds are freed only by the presence of God, which strengthens us with patience and perseverance. Let us plunge ourselves into the faith community and receive guidance and assurance of God's love. Let us commit to daily prayer that allows God to renew our minds so that we are freed to rejoice in doing God's will.

Self-Love

This is how we know what love is: Jesus Christ laid down his life for us. And we ought to lay down our lives for our brothers and sisters. If anyone has material possessions and sees a brother or sister in need but has no pity on them, how can the love of God be in that person? Dear children, let us not love with words or speech but with actions and in truth.

—1 JOHN 3:16–18 (NIV)

As disciples of our Lord Jesus, we are called to love our neighbor as ourselves, but do we truly understand what this means? What does it mean to love oneself? We see throughout scripture that much sin comes from loving ourselves too much. We must realize that there is a great difference between loving oneself as God intends and indulging in the selfish love that rages within us. Envy and lust drive our selfish love to covet what we don't have and hoard what we do. This is not the way, the truth, or the life Jesus instructed us to follow.

Our sinful love of self is probably the biggest obstacle to forming meaningful relationships with our God and our neighbor. The love of self and self alone leads us on a destructive path toward ease and pleasure at the expense of everyone around us. No matter whether we are wealthy or poor, we cannot see outside ourselves or realize how to express love to anyone as long as we continue on this selfish path. We must depend completely on God to show us how to love ourselves so that we can love others. Jesus gave us a clue when He said that we should treat others as we wish to be treated; therefore, we should examine our motives before almighty God and give thanks to the Holy Spirit for revealing our sorry state to us. Our hope of loving correctly comes as we more fully receive God's gracious gifts through Jesus and the Holy Spirit, for it is by receiving God's loving gift that we are redeemed from our selfishness. When we see our desperate situation, we should fall to our knees and pray for God's grace to strengthen us against our selfish desires and empty our hearts of lust and envy.

Dear disciple, let us surrender our will to our God so we can understand how to love ourselves correctly. Let us ask for divine wisdom, guidance, and strength so that we might turn from our animosity and resentment of others to selfless thoughts that bring reconciliation. Let us appreciate that our ability to know how to love God with all our being and how to love our neighbors as ourselves is tied directly to the acts of Jesus that empower us. Let us understand that being devoted followers of our Lord Jesus requires the pursuit of a love affair with God and being possessed by the Holy Spirit. Let us embrace God's presence so that we are enabled to truly love as our Creator intended and become useful in building the kingdom of God in the here and now.

Slander

Blessed are you when people insult you, persecute you and falsely say all kinds of evil against you because of me. Rejoice and be glad, because great is your reward in heaven, for in the same way they persecuted the prophets who were before you.

—MATTHEW 5:11–12 (NIV)

As disciples of our Lord Jesus, what should be our response when we are the victims of slander? Do we let ourselves succumb to righteous indignation and lash out with equally unkind words, or do we take a deep breath and rest calmly in the arms of Jesus? Jesus tells us that we should expect unpleasant insults and slanderous words from those around us. These attacks may come from those who have little regard for the ways of Jesus, but they may also come from those who profess to follow Jesus but disagree with our views on the matter. Insults, slanderous comments, and even violence seem to be the standard way of communication in our world today, affecting all aspects of life, but scripture says that we are to shun this behavior. Jesus goes on to say that we are actually blessed when we, His followers, are the targets of false and unkind words simply because we desire the will of God. This view of blessedness comes to us only when we choose an intimate connection with God and are willing to receive divine guidance and strength. When we choose to accept God's help, we are given supernatural power to respond to slander as Jesus teaches.

Slander comes in many forms, such as assaults on our character, attacks on our loved ones, or attacks on our belief system, which includes our understanding of what it means to be a follower of Jesus. Rather than letting our "blood boil" and saying things we later regret, we should know attacks are coming and be prepared by having God in the forefront of our every thought. If we know the teaching of Jesus intimately and are possessed by the Holy Spirit, we should not be bothered by what others say about us or our beliefs. We should understand the universal prevalence of weakness found in the human condition that drives us to act in evil ways unless we surrender our lives to God.

Dear disciple, let us remember that words are fleeting and that our peace of mind does not depend on the opinions of others. What others think of us does not change who we are as children of God, so let us hear our Heavenly Father call us to take the hand of Jesus and be filled with the Holy Spirit. Let us become captivated by the mysterious peace of God so that we can stand firmly against any verbal abuse. Let us refuse to abandon our source of life and strength and stand calmly in response to hurtful, false, and evil words, for this is our witness of Jesus to others. Let this unusual response be our goal in order to bring glory to our God and to demonstrate truth concerning God's kingdom.

Blessing Our Troubles

Consider it pure joy, my brothers and sisters, whenever you face trials of many kinds, because you know that the testing of your faith produces perseverance. Let perseverance finish its work so that you may be mature and complete, not lacking anything.

—JAMES 1:2–4 (NIV)

As disciples of our Lord Jesus, how do we interpret suffering? Do we feel God's blessings during our times of trouble, or do we get angry and ask, "Why me?" or "What did I do to deserve this?" When we see suffering in others, our usual response is to express sorrow or pity or to see injustice, but as we mature in our understanding of God's ways, we might be able to see a divine purpose behind the troubling challenges of life. It is difficult to hear the wisdom of our God or our faith community while we are wrestling with our troubles, for we are tempted to slip into despondency, depression, and despair. Even when we turn to our God for help, what do we expect to hear? How do we react when we hear scripture tell us that we should consider our troubles as blessings, for it appears that God allows troubles as means to draw us closer to Jesus and our faith community?

This can be a difficult lesson for us to learn. An unhelpful teaching that has existed for thousands of years is that if all is well, we must be right with God; if not, we must have done something wrong to deserve our troubles. Jesus and the New Testament authors speak strongly against this belief, saying that the troubles of life are universal and are not necessarily linked to our sin. Our troubles may be a result of our poor choices, but they are often seen as random and undeserved. Even as we struggle with life's troubles, we who have chosen to be guided along the path of Jesus by a faith community and have embraced scripture reading and prayer can expect to receive the loving and healing touch of God, which can sustain anyone through times of trouble. God's way of blessing us in the midst of our troubles can only be described as a marvelous mystery.

Dear disciple, let us understand that our ability to persevere through times of trouble comes only through an intimate love affair with our God and fellowship with our faith community. Our physical well-being and abundant possessions offer no protection from suffering, so let us allow God to transform our thinking to see our troubles as an opportunity to develop closer and deeper relationships and to see our need for God and the body of Christ. Let us pray continually to God for help in knowing this truth and, in humility and gratitude, embrace our God's presence for guidance in our times of distress. Let us trust and depend on our God and our faith community, for therein lies our hope and strength in our times of need.

Finding Divine Help

Simon Peter answered him, "Lord, to whom shall we go? You have the words of eternal life. We have come to believe and to know that you are the Holy One of God."

—JOHN 6:68–69 (NIV)

As disciples of our Lord Jesus, we read God's Holy Word to receive divine wisdom concerning how we are to become the true children of God. We hear Jesus tells us that our Father in heaven loves and cares for us but also desires our obedience to the divine covenant of love. We hear Jesus invite us to be yoked to Him by the Holy Spirit so that we receive relief from our burdens and guidance for our future. We hear scripture speak of God's gracious gift of salvation unto eternal life. Our response to these life-giving messages should be to embrace God's hope filled solutions for our troubled and weary lives. Scripture assures us that God is aware of our many needs and is delighted in guiding us to the provisional care found in our faith community. If we claim to be followers of Jesus, why would we choose to be so slow in seeking God's help in our times of trouble? Do we not hear Jesus say, "Come to me" (Matthew 11:28 NIV)? Do we not hear scripture say that God is ever present? Do we not understand that we find God's provision in the kingdom established by Jesus? Do we not know that our faith community is the representation of God's kingdom here on earth?

One of the great obstacles in following Jesus is trusting in the truth of His teachings. Having faith in Jesus only becomes real if our lives reflect what we say we believe, especially during times of trouble. So often we hide what is really going on before others because we feel embarrassed or guilty. We certainly don't want to appear weak to anyone. We must keep up appearances at all costs. It just isn't proper to allow others to think less of us. We can't let others know that we are just as needy as everyone else.

What a curse is our pride that separates us from our God and our loving faith community. What will it take for us to let go of pretenses and seek the mercies of our Creator? Do we really relish our anxieties and worries about the future? Do we enjoy embracing the cares of this world? How many times must we endure the same lesson that tries to teach us of our desperate need for God's help in all things?

Dear disciple, isn't it time we put away our childish ways and turn to the ways of Jesus? Isn't it time we embrace our God and learn the way of intimate love found only in the abiding presence of the Holy Spirit? Isn't it time we embrace our faith community, God's reality here on earth that encourages us and provides for us? Isn't it time to give up our doubting and questioning about unimportant things and trust completely in our God? Isn't it time we admit that God is our wisdom and strength? Let us wholeheartedly admit that God is our strength and our salvation and that we find rest in God alone for our troubled and weary souls.

Worldly Affection

No one can serve two masters. Either you will hate the one and love the other, or you will be devoted to the one and despise the other. You cannot serve both God and money.

—MATTHEW 6:24 (NIV)

Jesus replied, "No one who puts a hand to the plow and looks back is fit for service in the kingdom of God."

—LUKE 9:62 (NIV)

As disciples of our Lord Jesus, do we still find it difficult to dwell in God's presence? Do we still long for wisdom and guidance? Do we still seek understanding and revelation as we read scripture? All of these things are longed for by the follower of Jesus but are not easily attained unless we take Jesus seriously and follow His command to give up our worldly affections. We make progress on Jesus's path to life only by understanding our desperate need for God's grace in order to achieve our goal. Grace is a multifaceted gift that empowers us to see God's truth, receive God's wisdom, and enact the transformation necessary for us to be of use in God's kingdom. We must pray daily for God's gracious power to free us from our longing for comforts and relationships that have no godly merit.

Without God's help, we remain blind to the obstacles that impede our progress as Jesus's followers and, like the apostle Paul, desperately need God to remove the scales from our eyes. If we would only give God a chance, we would soon experience great rewards in terms of new insight, assurance, and strength for our journey. In abandoning ourselves to the will of God by being obedient to all the teachings and examples set by Jesus, we would be amazed at our ability to understand biblical passages that have befuddled us for years. We must recognize and admit that we are weak and need help in letting go of the things of earth. God cannot transform and renew our minds as long as we look backward at our darling lusts.

Dear disciple, knowledge may come quickly but discernment that leads to a transformed life takes time, hard work, and total commitment. We should see the difference between the learned, well-read, and brilliant scholar and the fruit-bearing, devout follower of Jesus. Although knowledge is very helpful, it is discernment flowing from divine sources that leads us to a useful life in the kingdom of God. Let us pray to God for help in understanding why it is so profitable to die to one's selfishness in order to be filled with all godliness. Let us fully embrace the love affair offered to each of us by our Heavenly Father through our Lord Jesus and the Holy Spirit. Let us be devoted to receiving godly revelation by fixing our eyes on Jesus. Let us then commit to flinging our sinful affections into the garbage heap so that we can be filled with divine understanding and bear spiritual fruit for God's glory.

My Time or God's

"Lord, remind me how brief my time on earth will be. Remind me that my days are numbered—how fleeting my life is. You have made my life no longer than the width of my hand. My entire lifetime is just a moment to you; at best, each of us is but a breath."

—PSALM 39:4–5 (NLT)

As disciples of our Lord Jesus, do we ask ourselves, "How much of my time is required to complete the journey?" This is a critical issue, for as long as we consider any of our time on earth as "my time," we can be assured that we are far from "being perfect, as our Father in heaven is perfect" (Matthew 5:48 NIV). This kind of thinking indicates that we have little interest in giving up our focus on self in order to attain the freedom that Jesus promises. If we do not comprehend the time and effort required to reach the goal of abiding in God, we will remain in a confused state of covetousness and continue seeking satisfaction and fulfillment in ungodly things. If we truly wish to find rest from our weary lives, we must give up our selfish desires and quit trying to partition our life into "my time" verses time I devote to God.

When we hear Jesus tell us that we should "count the cost" (Luke 14:28 NLT) of our journey, we should not despair at what is required of us but hear Jesus's invitation. It is truly a blessed event when we see that we cannot reach godly perfection alone! Even on the journey with Jesus at our side, we still ask many questions and pray many prayers concerning what is required of us. Thanks be to God for His loving-kindness, great mercy, and forgiveness concerning our stiff-necked thinking. This revelation should help us understand why baptism with the Holy Spirit and fire is required to purify us from our selfishness and complacency.

Dear disciple, let us remember that God created us, understands the cause for our faulty reasoning, and sends the Holy Spirit to draw us into intimacy. History tells us countless stories of saints who have overcome the entanglements of our enticing and sinful world to attain freedom for service in the kingdom of God. True discipleship is a full-time job, not something reserved for Sunday worship or the occasional prayer; therefore, let us commit to seeking God as the most important and valuable thing we can imagine. Let us abide in God as if our lives depend on this full-time practice, for this is the reality of a true disciple's life. Only then will we understand the joy of intimacy that comes from serving in God's kingdom.

Distractions

As Jesus and his disciples were on their way, he came to a village where a woman named Martha opened her home to him. She had a sister called Mary, who sat at the Lord's feet listening to what he said. But Martha was distracted by all the preparations that had to be made. She came to him and asked, "Lord, don't you care that my sister has left me to do the work by myself? Tell her to help me!" "Martha, Martha," the Lord answered, "you are worried and upset about many things, but few things are needed— or indeed only one. Mary has chosen what is better, and it will not be taken away from her."

—LUKE 10:38–42 (NIV)

As disciples of our Lord Jesus, even if we claim to have a great desire for the path of Jesus, we often find ourselves distracted by the frequent disruptions of life. Our focus can quickly shift from God's will to the satisfaction of our emotional needs to resolve the conflicts and pressures that weigh us down. When our sense of well-being is threatened, we try to protect it at all costs, but unless our minds are possessed by the presence of God, we usually respond to our dilemmas in a very un-Jesus like way. By allowing our unbridled emotions to override the Holy Spirit's guidance, we become like brute beasts that see any challenge to our well-being as a crisis.

Without God, any perceived happiness we might have is replaced with anger, remorse, sorrow, and even despair. Our devotion to Jesus is derailed by emergencies, our diligence is lost to exhaustion, and our communion with God implodes because of the vulgarities of life.

The only remedy to the distractions caused by the corruptions that invade our lives is to have the mind of Christ. The abiding presence of God allows us to recognize the foolishness of trying to satisfy our emotional unrest without the discernment provided by the Holy Spirit. Unless we fill our minds with the teachings of scripture, we cannot be empowered by God to stand unshaken and unwavering in the midst of the many uncertainties of life. Our emotional state is easily battered by our fickle world, and our loyalties remain divided unless we allow God to guide our thinking and our motives.

Dear disciple, are we not tired of letting our busyness and our undisciplined emotions drive our lives? Do we not yet recognize that the many shiny, delightful things of the world fail to satisfy the deep longings within us? Should we not resolve to keep our eyes fixed on Jesus, the author and perfecter of our faith, and allow God to guard our minds against these distractions? Should we not allow God to give us new vision to rightly see that worldly distractions cannot give us peace of mind? Let us stop trying to control our emotional turmoil alone and firmly commit to the path of Jesus. Let us pray for God to be our strength, our guide, and our satisfaction so that our emotions no longer rule over us or distract us from our true purpose of loving and serving in the kingdom of God.

God's Sweetness

Taste and see that the Lord is good; blessed is the one who takes refuge in him.

—PSALM 34:8 (NIV)

How sweet are your words to my taste, sweeter than honey to my mouth!

—PSALM 119:103 (NIV)

Have we, as disciples of our Lord Jesus, tasted the sweetness of our God, or does darkness still cloud our relationship? The disciple who has truly found God understands the sweetness of God's Word and cherishes every moment spent in communion with their Lord and Savior. We should see this as our ultimate goal as we hear Peter proclaim, "Where else can we go to find the words of eternal life?" (John 6:68 NIV). The sweet presence of God transforms our life situations, some of which we find objectionable, into blessings that actually bring us great delight. God's presence allows our troubled hearts to be filled with peace and joy that enables us to serve and share the love of Jesus in hard places. Nothing can satisfy us for long unless the loving and gracious presence of God transforms the now moments of life for the good. The one who is truly satisfied in life is the one who delights in God's sweet presence.

Once we have tasted the sweetness of God, we know we have found the true path of life that empowers us to reject any vain worldly way in order to satisfy our lusty flesh. Darkness and death are the rewards for worldly solutions, so why would we continue in their practice? Should we not pray for our vision to be enlightened by the sweetness of God's divine truth? We must be led to see the stark difference between creature and Creator, between the eternal Light of God and the dull light of man if we are ever to enjoy the sweetness of our God. Only then will we clearly hear the Holy Spirit's call to glorify God by reflecting the light of Jesus.

Dear disciple, we must not let ourselves be led astray by our uncrucified self. Let us pray that God's eternal light would enlighten the inmost recesses of our hearts by cleansing our minds with the Holy Spirit. Let us admit that our lusts still lurk in the kingdom of self that is waiting to spring forth and tempt us away from our God and our faith community. Let us turn to our Creator and let God's sweet presence become our all in all. Let us relish God's sweetness and proclaim, "Thine is the kingdom, the power, and the glory forever and ever." Let us cherish God's glorious gift and rest assured that our refuge, our strength, and our hope are found in nothing else.

Security

Trust in the Lord with all your heart and lean not on your own understanding; in all your ways submit to him, and he will make your paths straight. Do not be wise in your own eyes; fear the Lord and shun evil.

—PROVERBS 3:5–7 (NIV)

As disciples of our Lord Jesus, are we still guilty of seeking security from the kingdom of self rather than the kingdom of God? Surely by now we realize that life is unpredictable and that the only reliable security we have comes from God. We must face the fact that we dwell among stiff-necked people with little if any regard for God and, as a result, we are subject to attack when we least expect it. We must daily remind ourselves that God is our refuge and strength, our ever-present help in times of trouble. We must become possessed by the presence of God every moment of every day or risk losing our way and succumbing to our fears and anxieties that tempt us to turn to our former stiffed-necked, sinful ways.

Seeking momentary relief from our troubles found in worldly solutions pale in comparison to the everlasting rest found in God. Are we not yet convinced that Jesus is the way? Have we not read scripture and said that we believe its truth? Have we not proclaimed to the world that we are followers of Jesus and that we trust God in all things? If these statements are true, why then are we so weak when faced with the troubles of the world? The great cloud of witnesses tells us that the blessed peace of God is ours if we would believe with our whole being and allow the Holy Spirit to recreate us. With God's abiding help, it *is* possible to cheerfully undergo all labors and sorrows, temptations and trials, anxieties, weaknesses, necessities, injuries, slanders, rebukes, humiliations, confusions, corrections, and contempt found in this life. Our love affair with God is the answer to life's difficulties.

Dear disciple, successfully overcoming the labors we must endure in this brief life requires patience and perseverance, which come only from God. We may think we are clever, but life proves us to be the fool unless we place all our confidence in our Lord and Savior. Let us love the Lord God with our whole being and lean not on our own understanding. Let us receive courage from our God and be assured of our victory in Christ Jesus. Let us dwell in the Holy Spirit so that we are empowered to let Jesus live through us and allow others to have a glimpse of God's kingdom.

The Vain Judgments of Humankind

It is God's will that your honorable lives should silence those ignorant people who make foolish accusations against you. For you are free, yet you are God's slaves, so don't use your freedom as an excuse to do evil. Respect everyone, and love the family of believers. Fear God, and respect the king.

—1 PETER 2:15–17 (NLT)

As disciples of our Lord Jesus, we should no longer be upset by the judgments of others if we have a firm grasp of God's truth and are truly living out the way of Jesus. Our conscience should be clear before others, but if the judgment of others still causes us emotional turmoil, we must ask ourselves, "Why?" People say many things based on their biases and prejudices, but if people's "truth" is not based on godly truth, why should we be concerned with or put faith in what they have to say? Should our goal in life be to change our beliefs and behavior to please people or to please God? The world is full of many so-called "truths," making it impossible to agree with or to please everyone, but if we are anchored in God's wisdom and have received the mind of Christ, we should understand as Jesus does what is in human beings. We should no longer be concerned about conforming to the ways of the world and instead be focused on conforming to the way that leads to eternal life.

Paul's life is such a good example of the way of Jesus in that he never let the prejudiced and abusive judgments of others change him in any way. He labored constantly for the edification and salvation of others, committing all he had to God's glory. With great humility, Paul trusted God to be his defender, refuge, and strength through all that he suffered for the name of Jesus.

Dear disciple, as children of God, children of the promise, why should we be upset by or fear the vain judgment of mortal humans? Are we not here on earth for but a short while? Are not the uninspired words of human beings like the morning fog that is soon gone and forgotten? Do not cruel words and prejudiced judgments eventually cause more injury to the deliverer than the receiver? Have we not heard scripture warn us to fear God and not the judgments of men and women, for is not God ultimately responsible for our well-being? Let us remember that judgment and justice against our enemies are God's business, not ours, for no one can escape the judgment of the Creator. When we see unjust judgment or suffer unkind words from others, we should remember the evil source from whence it comes and pray for God to intervene for us and for those affected. Let us commit to being the hands and feet of Christ for the unjustly afflicted. Let us pray to our Rock and Redeemer to fill us with the Holy Spirit's mighty strength to persevere against the vain judgment of human beings and for deliverance from such evil.

Accepting God's Freedom

Jesus said to the people who believed in him, "You are truly my disciples if you remain faithful to my teachings. And you will know the truth, and the truth will set you free."

—JOHN 8:31–32 (NLT)

Do we, as disciples of Jesus, really understand the freedom Jesus encourages us to accept? Do we realize what we must give up in order to truly receive this gift from our God? Those who have gone before us testify that we must give up our willful self and our selfish attachments in order to gain access to our God's wisdom and power. We may from time to time experience moments of the freedom Jesus promises, but if we really want to experience total freedom, we must irrevocably surrender our will and take on the will of God.

Are we who say we want to become faithful followers of Jesus willing to ask, "Lord, to obtain this freedom You speak of, what exactly are You asking me to give up, and how do I accomplish this?" Jesus's answer confirmed by the saints that surround us is to continually, in matters great and small, stop relying on our own judgment and turn to God for guidance; otherwise, God's promised freedom from self will remain elusive, and our commitment to the needs of others only sporadic. We should realize the magnitude of the challenge before us that requires us to seek not only God's presence in prayer and scripture reading but also God's presence and guidance found in our faithful community. We cannot find Jesus's promised freedom alone! If we wish to enjoy the liberty of a pure heart found in God's grace filled friendship, we must give up the right to our selfish ways, sit at the foot of Jesus's cross, and daily sacrifice our will in order to receive God's will. Only then will we become an acceptable holy vessel into which God can pour the Holy Spirit, which empowers us to embrace this new freedom. Unless we resolve to adhere to this path, we cannot enjoy full abiding with God or receive the full impact of God's gracious spiritual gifts.

Dear disciple, let us refuse to waver in our quest for spiritual freedom. Let us commit to the abandonment of self so that we might receive this heavenly treasure. We must daily meditate in God's presence on this matter, in good times and bad; otherwise, we should not expect to receive God's freedom that brings peace of mind. Let us abandon any demands or conditions in our loyalty to God so that we might freely receive God's gracious gift that frees us to give freely to others. To possess the freedom offered by Jesus, we must trust purely and without hesitation in God's provision of grace that surrounds us and frees us from our dark and sinful thinking. Our goal should be to desire the gift of freedom above all else, to be stripped naked as Jesus on the cross, to die to self, and to live forever for and in the presence of our Triune God. This is true freedom. A life that is free from all vain imaginations, all wicked thoughts, and all worries, anxieties, and fears. All that remains is for us to experience the transforming love of God, the living water, which frees us to bring blessings in all that we say and do.

Priorities and Treasures

Do not store up for yourselves treasures on earth, where moth and rust consume and where thieves break in and steal; but store up for yourselves treasures in heaven, where neither moth nor rust consumes and where thieves do not break in and steal. For where your treasure is, there your heart will be also.

—MATTHEW 6:19–21 (NRSV)

As disciples of our Lord Jesus, we are asked to reprioritize our lives so that we might be free to serve in the kingdom of God. The requirement for this mighty task is a rightly ordered mind concerning the things that occupy our time. We should hear Jesus tell us that to be inwardly free, we must have mastery over everything that consumes our thinking. To this point, we must consider whether we are in control of or are controlled by our possessions. Are we the master and director of our actions, or are we simply a slave to our desires? If we are truly God's children, we should be able to rise above temporal present things in order to engage in things eternal. Our eyes should be filled with the light of the Holy Spirit so that we put things in their proper perspective as ordained by our God.

It takes much time spent with God and our faith community to gain the discernment required to be content with who we are and what we have. Those with carnal eyes are forever dissatisfied with the status quo, spending precious time and resources pursuing the newer, shinier thing rather than devoting themselves to what builds the kingdom of God. Loving relationships with our God and each other should consume our time above all other things. What is required of us is self-control, which the apostle Paul reminds us is a spiritual gift. Should this not be a clue that we remain powerless to follow through with the teachings of Jesus unless we pray for and receive this most valuable gift?

Dear disciple, if we are to be free to do the things that please God, we must know well the things that draw us away from our Creator, recognize when these things start to cloud our thinking, and then run to our God for help in resisting their attack. If we still feel too weak to resist, we must turn to our brothers and sisters in Christ for their help as well. Let us resolve to abide in our Heavenly Father, our Lord Jesus, and the Holy Spirit, for we have no other hope for victory over the distractions that would rule our lives. Let us give up our earthly treasures for heavenly ones by taking refuge in our God and humbly pleading for divine aid in overcoming our addictions. Let us allow God to rightly prioritize our lives by renewing our minds with the will of Jesus so that we can truly become God's covenant people. Let us become possessed by the Holy Spirit so that we can demonstrate what is truly important to our broken and troubled world.

Patience in Prayer

How long, Lord? Will you forget me forever? How long will you hide your face from me? How long must I wrestle with my thoughts and day after day have sorrow in my heart? How long will my enemy triumph over me? Look on me and answer, Lord my God. Give light to my eyes, or I will sleep in death.

—PSALM 13:1–3 (NIV)

We also pray that you will be strengthened with all his glorious power so you will have all the endurance and patience you need. May you be filled with joy, always thanking the Father. He has enabled you to share in the inheritance that belongs to his people, who live in the light. For he has rescued us from the kingdom of darkness and transferred us into the Kingdom of his dear Son, who purchased our freedom and forgave our sins.

—COLOSSIANS 1:11–14 (NLT)

As disciples of our Lord Jesus, we are instructed to bring all of our concerns to God in prayer: our cares, our worries, our problems, our confusion, our anger, our guilt, our temptations, our sins, etc. The list can go on and on. We may experience comfort and relief in short order, but in most cases, answers or resolutions to our problems are often delayed, sometimes seemingly beyond our ability to bear. We may say that we commit our cares to God but are often guilty of trying to tell God how to fix them. We must learn that committing something to God's care requires us to let go of it and wait patiently for a divine solution. After all, don't we believe that God has our best interest at heart even though we can't see the solution to our problem?

We must admit that we are not very patient in waiting. Our culture has trained us to expect immediate results for our problems. We say, "I want it my way, and I want it now!" Our impatience is part of the human condition from the beginning. The phrase "How long?" in reference to God's delayed help occurs over one hundred times in scripture, which shows how uncomfortable and impatient we are with our uncertain future.

Many times we enter God's presence with no idea as to how God can rescue us or resolve our troubles. Unfortunately, we are so good at rationalizing that we don't remember all the things we did to get ourselves into our present state and can't see the path required for God to resolve our situation. Even if our situation is not our fault, we must trust God and our faith community to sustain us for the journey. We must come to grips with the fact that our solutions tend to be selfish in nature and usually bring only temporary relief.

Dear disciple, let us understand that patience is not some power we possess. Patience is a spiritual gift from God, a power that comes only from abiding in God's presence. Let us become rock-solid in our assurance of knowing that our God loves us, forgives us, and wants what is best for us. Let us resolve to let go of our problems and cast our care upon Jesus even to the point of allowing Him to carry us along the way. Let us rely on God and the indwelling Holy Spirit to strengthen us for every task. Let us be willing to be formed into unwavering instruments that can withstand any circumstance. Let us learn to trust our God in all things so we can stop asking, "How long?"

The Mysterious Love of God

When I look at the night sky and see the work of your fingers—the moon and the stars you set in place—what are mere mortals that you should think about them, human beings that you should care for them? Yet you made them only a little lower than God and crowned them with glory and honor. You gave them charge of everything you made, putting all things under their authority.

—PSALM 8:3–6 (NLT)

As disciples of our Lord Jesus, we should stand in constant amazement of the fact that despite our unfaithfulness, God loves us and desires an intimate relationship with us. As God reveals the ugliness of our sin, we may find it hard to believe that God's grace is freely given to anyone just because they are willing to receive the forgiving, redeeming touch of Jesus. Surely we must do something to earn God's love and favor. Or do we feel a sense of entitlement and think that by claiming to believe in Jesus, God should be at our beck and call? Since we so easily misunderstand the mysterious love of God, we should commit to examining our lives in God's presence and ask repeatedly for the Holy Spirit to reveal the truth of scripture concerning this amazing fact. We desperately need God to empower us in order to respond to and act accordingly to the love of God. We should shout hallelujah because of the unimaginable love of God demonstrated by the acts of Jesus our Savior, but we often cringe when we hear that we are of little value to the kingdom of God unless Jesus becomes the center of our lives. It is a difficult task to understand the mysterious ways of God's love. In fact, we don't really understand what love is until we receive and embrace God's grace and the required divine wisdom that comes from the presence of the Holy Spirit.

By abiding is God's presence, we should become more and more assured of God's love for us, and as we allow divine wisdom to transform our ignorant minds, we begin to see that our goal is to become more like our Savior, who is forever the same, always good, just, holy, doing justice and mercy in all things, and loving unconditionally. Like Peter, we may be eager at first but are so prone to doubt and confusion that we sink beneath the waves unless we grasp the hand of Jesus and plead for Holy Spirit power. The sole purpose for our creation is to live pleasing our God by infusing love into all we do. True love is a spiritual gift from God. We are incapable of true love without this gift. If we choose not to receive this gift, we risk hearing our Lord Jesus accuse us of being lukewarm and threaten to spit us out of His mouth (Revelation 3:16 NIV).

Dear disciple, let us give thanks to our Creator God who sees something beautiful in us worth saving despite our vain, weak, and erratic lives. Let us give God the Father, God the Son, and God the Holy Spirit all honor and glory and accept the fact that God has found us worthy. Let us always remember that it is God who makes us holy and enables us by the Holy Spirit to truly love. Love is a spiritual gift. Let us understand that we are nothing unless the mysterious love of God fills us and makes us whole.

Honor

I do not receive honor from men. But I know you, that you do not have the love of God in you. I have come in My Father's name, and you do not receive Me; if another comes in his own name, him you will receive. How can you believe, who receive honor from one another, and do not seek the honor that comes from the only God?

—JOHN 5:41–44 (NKJV)

Then he said to them, "You like to appear righteous in public, but God knows your hearts. What this world honors is detestable in the sight of God."

—LUKE 16:15 (NLT)

As disciples of our Lord Jesus, we should regularly ask ourselves if we still crave recognition and honor. Do we understand what it means to be honored, and do we desire to receive honor from humankind or from our God? We might define honor as special recognition bestowed on a person who is greatly admired and respected because of their achievements. Honor is something given and something received, but scripture tell us that the pursuit of honor should never be our motive in anything we do. When our actions are motivated by the desire to receive honor and recognition for our good works, we should hear Jesus tell us to stop chasing such vanity! The desire to receive recognition and honor is driven by our pride and envy and is never pleasing to God. If our desire is to make progress along the path of righteousness, we must repent of this vanity and wholeheartedly pursue humility.

There are times when we receive unexpected honor in serving God, but we must receive this honor with humility; otherwise, our undisciplined emotions will inflame our prideful minds to become puffed up as we say to ourselves, "Look at me. Am I not great?" If we allow ourselves to be driven by a desire to impress and please people, we miss the mark of discipleship and fall short of our calling as God's holy people. The desire for self-glory is ever present and requires us to give the Holy Spirit the freedom necessary to conquer this prideful vice within us. Jesus has commanded us to serve with an attitude of humility in all we say and do. When we receive honor, we should receive it with humble gratitude, knowing our actions were guided and empowered by the presence of the Holy Spirit for God's honor and glory.

Dear disciple, let us give up the ways of arrogance whose unattractive appearance is haughty and bigheaded. Let us remember that all we are and all we have is a divine gift to be used for God's glory. Arrogance is an ugly, slow-acting poison that subtly invades our minds, blinding us and steering us from the path of discipleship. Our highest honor comes from pleasing our God in kingdom service while knowing that all we say and do is to be a representation of Jesus. Let us look forward to receiving God's greatest honor as we hear Jesus say, "Well done, good and faithful servant" (Matthew 25:21 NIV).

Peace Is Not Found apart from God

In my distress I prayed to the Lord, and the Lord answered me and set me free. The Lord is for me, so I will have no fear. What can mere people do to me? Yes, the Lord is for me; he will help me. I will look in triumph at those who hate me. It is better to take refuge in the Lord than to trust in people. It is better to take refuge in the Lord than to trust in princes.

—PSALM 118:5–9 (NLT)

As disciples of our Lord Jesus, do we still find ourselves consumed by the secular affairs of the world while hoping that someone somehow will do something to bring us peace? We are sensual creatures driven to satisfy our desires, and this reality makes it very hard for us to give up our lust for the things of this world and those who provide them. Our bodies and minds are programed to enjoy all that God has created for us, but when we devote more time and energy to satisfying ourselves with things created than to the worship of our God, we are guilty of idolatry and have broken our covenant promise to our God. Putting our trust in created things and worldly people for the peace of mind we long for is a vain pursuit. Isn't it time for us to give up the hypocritical life of giving God lip service while we covet security from our fellow beings and our possessions?

Isn't it time for us to trust in the assurances of scripture, which tells us that salvation is not found in man but in God alone?

Why is it so hard to hear God's plea to turn and practice the spiritual disciplines of study, prayer, and community service alongside our fellow disciples to strengthen our minds against our selfish will so that God's will prevails in our lives? Shouldn't we receive and embrace God's revelation of the truth concerning our salvation and be empowered to show love, compassion, forgiveness, and generosity as demonstrated by our Lord Jesus? It is in these acts that we find peace, for the peace of God cannot be found in any earthly minded creature or created thing.

Dear disciple, let us give up our puny faith and look to our God to obtain the divine understanding necessary to have complete assurance in scriptural truth. Even though we cannot entirely understand or adequately explain the peace of God, we can live out the reality of God's truth knowing that our Savior's promises never fail. Let us give up our worries and fears that burden our lives and claim the assurances of God for ourselves. Are we not tired of hearing Jesus say, "You of little faith" (Matthew 8:26 NIV)? Let us trust our God completely and rest assured in the reality of the gift of peace.

Vain Worldly Knowledge

Timothy, guard what has been entrusted to you. Avoid the profane chatter and contradictions of what is falsely called knowledge; by professing it some have missed the mark as regards the faith. Grace be with you.

—1 TIMOTHY 6:20–21 (NRSV)

As disciples of our Lord Jesus, have we received the guiding gift of godly discernment, or do we continue to consume the abundant vain worldly wisdom that corrupts our thinking? We must confess that we are easily swayed by the smooth and eloquent talk of others, unless we are grounded in God's truth; otherwise, we are ill prepared to deal with those skilled in persuasive argument. Scripture clearly tells us to be on guard against would be deceivers gifted with fine-sounding and subtle words. Of course there is much wisdom in the world that is useful in gaining practical life skills, and when used correctly, these skills can be very helpful in building the kingdom of God; unfortunately, we often fail to involve the Holy Spirit's guidance in the use of this knowledge and thus allow our selfish motives to guide our decisions. Our Creator has given us minds with great reasoning power, but as our knowledge base increases, we must be committed to allowing God's help in discerning what is true and useful. As followers of Jesus, we must understand that excluding God from our reasoning process places us in grave danger.

We are by nature curious creatures that must satisfy our minds by delving into many things, but until our minds are anchored in God's truth, we will continue to be subject to the slippery words of the world that darken our minds and dull our conscience against our created purpose of loving our God and neighbor above all else. How long will we choose to walk in darkness before we fully embrace the Holy Spirit, which guides us and empowers us to persevere in kingdom service?

Dear disciple, let us remember that it is God who gives wisdom to our knowledge and vision for what is good, right, and true. Even as we pursue secular knowledge for our benefit, let us never stop hungering for the kingdom of God. In all our study, let us cling to the righteous path of Jesus and desire nothing apart from Him. Let us never lose focus on the fact that our knowledge must be possessed of love, mercy, forgiveness, and generosity; otherwise, our understanding of the mystery of the kingdom of God will continue to be veiled in darkness.

Concerns and Worries

Still others, like seed sown among thorns, hear the word; but the worries of this life, the deceitfulness of wealth and the desires for other things come in and choke the word, making it unfruitful.

—MARK 4:18–19 (NIV)

As disciples of our Lord Jesus, do we truly understand our Master's teachings concerning the futility of worry? Do we continue to struggle with the many uncertainties that daily assault our lives? We should recognize that worry robs us of our peace of mind and hinders our progress as disciples. When worry consumes our thinking, we become prisoners of an unfruitful mind that prevents us from pursuing a life pleasing to God. Why do we let worry rule over us when we know and have probably experienced the fact that worry never changes the outcome of any situation? The unfortunate answer to this question is because we have a puny faith that puts little trust in our God's providential care. The solution to worry is not found in praying for God to solve our problems while we hide from the world. We must seek God's presence in a community of faith skilled in godly wisdom, discernment, and compassionate listening. This is the body of Christ that gives us guidance and encouragement in our times of need.

Scripture clearly describes the necessity of being part of a godly community from beginning to end. There should be no need for worry if we are part of a community focused on living out God's covenant of love. Our prideful minds tempt us to go it alone, thinking it is up to us to fix our problems. Rather than trying to find security in the temporal things of the world, shouldn't we be fully participating in a covenant love community? We labor and fret over things of little or no value and allow our minds to be consumed with the possibility of their loss. Without a faith community to lead us into holiness, we will let worry separate us from our God to the detriment of our souls. A helpful guide is the Serenity Prayer of Reinhold Niebuhr, which entreats God to help us accept the things we cannot change, courage to change the things we can, and wisdom to know the difference.

Dear disciple, let us commit to becoming free from worry over the concerns of life. Let us see the damage worry causes to our love affair with our God. Let us repent of this deadly sin and turn away from the false security found in the temporal solutions set forth by humankind. Let us examine our relationships and our possessions before God and allow Holy Spirit power to be our comfort and solution for our fears. Let us resolve to embrace the peace found in the presence of God and our faith community, for it is here that God's covenant love brings consolation and rest for our troubled and weary souls.

Persuasive Words

We must no longer be children, tossed to and fro and blown about by every wind of doctrine, by people's trickery, by their craftiness in deceitful scheming. But speaking the truth in love, we must grow up in every way into him who is the head, into Christ, from whom the whole body, joined and knit together by every ligament with which it is equipped, as each part is working properly, promotes the body's growth in building itself up in love.

—EPHESIANS 4:14–16 (NRSV)

As disciples of our Lord Jesus, have we committed ourselves to the wisdom of God as our primary source of truth? Our thinking has certainly been shaped by our education, and the world would convince us to place our hope in the cleverness of humankind for solutions, but let us not forget how often we have been deceived by persuasive talk even from those we thought trustworthy. When things go badly, we are left feeling disappointed and perplexed as to who we can trust. How long will it take us to admit that we are too easily led astray unless God is present to guard our minds from the ways of the world? Why is it so hard for us to entrust our minds to the ways of our Lord Jesus? Don't we profess that Jesus is the rock and foundation upon which we live?

Even though we are created in God's image, we must remember

that our human condition makes us vulnerable to being made the fool. For this reason, it is critical for us to find godly saints in which we can confide! We must encourage each other to stay faithful to our God and seek Holy Spirit guidance daily to steel our minds against attack. Have we not had enough of paying the price for poor judgment because of our lack of discipline? Are we not slow to believe scripture that assures us of the certainty of attack from those with a crafty tongue? Should we not pray to God for discernment and protection from enticing speech that leads us astray?

Dear disciple, let us commit to finding our way in the world by abiding in our God, for there is no other certainty in creation. Let us understand that there is no other way toward a confident life in God's kingdom than the one taught and demonstrated by Jesus. Let us become armed with God's truth and rely on the Holy Spirit to clarify the motive behind the truth of others. Let us also shun the use of clever words simply to impress others but be faithful in proclaiming the good news of Jesus in simple words and good deeds. What a grievous sin it is to misrepresent our God to others. Let us be faithful image bearers of our Creator who has entrusted us with the keys to the kingdom of God.

Words That Challenge Us

We know that we have come to know him if we keep his commands. Whoever says, "I know him," but does not do what he commands is a liar, and the truth is not in that person.

—1 JOHN 2:3–4 (NIV)

When he was accused by the chief priests and the elders, he gave no answer. Then Pilate asked him, "Don't you hear the testimony they are bringing against you?" But Jesus made no reply, not even to a single charge—to the great amazement of the governor.

—MATTHEW 27:12–14 (NIV)

As disciples of our Lord Jesus, how do we respond when others cast harsh judgment upon us? Do their words affirm a deep truth we have chosen to ignore? Do their accusations touch a nerve that causes us to reach into our bag of excuses? Even though the words of others cause us no physical damage, they do challenge us and, if we are honest, often convict us of hypocrisy. Before we respond to the judgments of others, we should be willing to consult our God for divine discernment as to the truth concerning what we have heard. This is a difficult task that goes against our very nature of self-defense and self-preservation. Until we allow God to enlighten our minds, we will defend our corrupt image at all cost to prove the offending person wrong. Why are we so slow to see that our perceived self-image is not the desired image for which God created us?

Our time in prayer, study, and fellowship should be focused on knowing the truth about ourselves and our need for the presence of the Holy Spirit for guidance in listening and responding to the challenges of others. It takes the spiritual gift of humility for us to admit that we are often guilty of the judgment we hear, and this point of view comes only from the abiding presence of God, who is our strength and help in these times of distress.

It takes even more humility to bear the pain of false and slanderous words for the sake of God. Did not our Savior set the example for us as He endured the hateful words of His accusers? If our response falls short of this, we must admit that sinful ways are still alive within us. We must face the fact that we want everyone's admiration and only want to hear positive things about ourselves, but Jesus would tell us to be willing to receive both good and hurtful words from others, for this is the required path for us to become humble servants in the kingdom of God.

Dear disciple, let us look deeply inside ourselves to see if we are guilty of the judgment we receive from others. Let us lean on the presence of God for help in examining what we hear from others when emotions run high and venomous words well up in our mouths. Let us admit our weakness in this area and turn to our God for help in training us to respond with patient listening. Let us invite the Holy Spirit to guard our mouths and quiet our souls, knowing that only God can reveal the truth in what we hear. Let us learn well what is required to abide continually in God's presence so that we can respond with gentleness and understanding to our accusers' words for we know that they are struggling with the same flawed human condition. Let us allow God to arm us with the spiritual gifts of love, compassion, and forgiveness so that we can endure whatever may come for the sake of God's holy name.

Bearing Our Trials

Dear friends, do not be surprised at the fiery ordeal that has come on you to test you, as though something strange were happening to you. But rejoice inasmuch as you participate in the sufferings of Christ, so that you may be overjoyed when his glory is revealed. If you are insulted because of the name of Christ, you are blessed, for the Spirit of glory and of God rests on you.

—1 PETER 4:12–14 (NIV)

As disciples of our Lord Jesus, we must hear and understand the teachings of scripture concerning the many trials and sorrows we may face serving in God's kingdom. As we struggle internally with our trials, whatever they may be, we must grow in our faith and rest assured that Jesus has won the victory for us by overcoming the world. So how does Jesus's victory help us in our trials? First, we must ask ourselves if we really believe that Jesus is an ever-present source of strength and consolation in our time of need. Next, we must ask if we have joined a faith community so that we can experience God's consoling and encouraging touch through their hands. Unfortunately, many tend to think that trials must simply be endured while on earth for they believe God's consolation is reserved for heaven or for the future coming of Jesus. As disciples, we must grow to see that Jesus is offering His help in the here and now!

We are given spiritual practices for personal training to strengthen ourselves so that we can bear our trials with hope, but this is only part of the answer. If we stubbornly hold to a "self-help" attitude in prayer and meditation, Bible study, and devotional reading, we will fail in our quest. The key to our perseverance in overcoming our trials is found only when we follow Jesus into a faith community. Without the faith community, we have no chance of understanding how desperately we need others to help us see and live out God's truth.

Going it alone springs from pride and arrogance, which clouds our minds from the real truth. We are prone to misread or misunderstand scripture or to miss the truth entirely by ourselves. God calls us into community for it is our faith community that guides us, encourages us, and keeps us strong in our times of need. Community enables us to join with Jesus in saying, "I have overcome the world" (John 16:33 NIV). We no longer have to say, "Who shall deliver me from this body of death" (Romans 7:24 NKJV) as we wrestle with whatever trial we face. It is in community that we find assurance of the reality of the kingdom of God in the here and now. It is in community that we strengthen our faith in God's promises and our hope in things eternal.

Dear disciple, it is when we are in our deepest trial that we need our faith community to help us lift our eyes to behold our God. Our faith community helps us see how God strengthened all the saints who have gone before us by binding them into communities where they became the hands and feet of Jesus to each other. We truly take comfort in the victory of Jesus when we are part of His body, our faith community. It is here that we find God's assurances and consolations that bring us peace of mind in all circumstances.

When Life Turns Dark

Lord, do not rebuke me in your anger or discipline me in your wrath. Have mercy on me, Lord, for I am faint; heal me, Lord, for my bones are in agony. My soul is in deep anguish. How long, Lord, how long? Turn, Lord, and deliver me; save me because of your unfailing love. Among the dead no one proclaims your name. Who praises you from the grave? I am worn out from my groaning. All night long I flood my bed with weeping and drench my couch with tears.

—PSALM 6:1–6 (NIV)

As disciples of our Lord Jesus, we hear of the grace and mercy of our God and often experience the joy of the Holy Spirit's presence, but our journey is sometimes plagued with what has been called the dark night of the soul. From time to time, we all suffer trials and hardships that darken our thinking. Rather than seeing ourselves as children of God, we see ourselves as the exiled sons and daughters of Eve. Our days seem bitter and tedious and full of grief and distress. We may feel defiled by many sins, ensnared in many passions, enslaved by many fears, and burdened with many cares. We may be distracted by many curiosities and entangled in many vanities, surrounded by many errors and wearied by many labors, oppressed by temptations, and tormented by want. We cry out, "When will these evil days end?"

We may turn to God in frustration or anger and say, "When will You free me from my misery? When will You restore my joy? When will I enjoy Your presence?" We long for true liberty from every grievance of mind and body. We want undisturbed and secure inward peace despite all outward turmoil. If only we could gaze into the face of Jesus and feel His healing caress. If only He would transform and protect our minds from all distractions and evil influences. If only we could see the kingdom of God and be assured of its promises. If only …

Dear disciple, it is during these times that we most need the assurances of our God and the encouraging guidance of our faith community, for therein lies our rescue. It is the holy community of God that listens to us, loves us, and holds us close as we struggle to survive through these hard times. It is our brothers and sisters in Christ who reassure us that God has not forsaken us and that our relationship will be restored one day stronger than ever. We must remember that even in our darkest hour, we are loved and we never have to travel this life alone. Let us resolve to never forget that our God is found among the faithful followers of Jesus who will never leave us or forsake us. Let us be assured that we are God's dearly loved children, whom He desires to shelter in the shadow of His wings. Let us leave our arrogance and pride behind and run into the arms of Jesus found in His holy community. Let us seek the presence of God and allow Jesus's gentle, loving, healing touch to release us from the bitterness of our souls.

Where Is God When We Struggle?

But I pray to you, Lord, in the time of your favor; in your great love, O God, answer me with your sure salvation. Rescue me from the mire, do not let me sink; deliver me from those who hate me, from the deep waters. Do not let the floodwaters engulf me or the depths swallow me up or the pit close its mouth over me.

—PSALM 69:13–15 (NIV)

As disciples of our Lord Jesus, how faithful are we when troubles drag on day after day? When resolutions to our struggles are nowhere in sight, are we tempted to falter in our relationships with God and those we love? Our troubled minds may turn from pleasing God to the satisfaction of our own selfish needs that can lead us down a dangerous path, resulting in alienation from the very help we need. Struggles often awaken our desire to pursue former sinful things we thought we had overcome. When we find our minds dwelling on earthly rather than heavenly treasures, we should recognize what is happening, stop, repent, and turn to our God and our faith community for help in restoring righteousness. Thank goodness we have Jesus as our advocate who understands how and why we think and act as we do. He comes to us with compassion and mercy and provides us strength and guidance before we collapse under our corrupt thinking. Is it not amazing how temporal delights never cease to call to us, especially when we struggle?

Scripture reveals that God uses a refining fire to cleanse our thinking; therefore, we must learn to welcome God's fire to consume our sinful desires if we ever hope to overcome that which burns within us. We must constantly ask the Holy Spirit to be our wisdom and strength in overcoming our weakness. We must seriously commit to the path of humility and receive godly power to achieve holiness. We must understand that God knows our longings, for God hears our frequent sighs and greatly desires to bring us relief. God understands our desire for eternal rest and peace, but God would say to us that our hour has not yet come and that there remains for us more labor for the kingdom and, perhaps, more trials to endure.

Dear disciple, God has told us to expect trying times but assures us of Holy Spirit consolation both now and forevermore. Like our Lord Jesus, we must be willing to humbly bow to the will of others without complaining, all the while relying on the abiding presence of our God to enable us to perform what is required to our best ability. Let us find our pleasure in faithfully pleasing our God by bringing honor and glory to the name of Jesus. Let us remember that true joy is found only in our God and our faith community for this is where we find comfort and strength for every required task and trial we face. Let us rejoice when finally we can say that God has become our complete satisfaction in all things.

My All Comes from God

Don't be deceived, my dear brothers and sisters. Every good and perfect gift is from above, coming down from the Father of the heavenly lights, who does not change like shifting shadows. He chose to give us birth through the word of truth, that we might be a kind of first-fruits of all he created.

—JAMES 1:16–18 (NIV)

Ask and it will be given to you; seek and you will find; knock and the door will be opened to you. For everyone who asks receives; the one who seeks finds; and to the one who knocks, the door will be opened.

—MATTHEW 7:7–8 (NIV)

As disciples of our Lord Jesus, are we willing to receive all that God would give us? Are we willing to admit that everything we possess, whether it be material, physical, or spiritual, comes from our God? More importantly, do we even know of the good things God desires to give us or of the persistence required from us in asking? Our journey with God usually begins with requests for many fleshy desires, but as we mature in our faith and understanding of God's desires for us, our prayer life turns toward more spiritual and eternal matters. We begin to see that as sinners, we have no merit before our God and must rely completely on God's love for us despite our sinful condition. We must come to grasp the concept of God's grace extended to us through our Savior Jesus if we are to appreciate the depth of this revealed truth. The unfathomable love poured out on us by our Heavenly Father through the Holy Spirit should bring us to our knees and cause us to give God all thanks and praise. It is at this point that we must decide whether we will receive and embrace the divine gift of love and be empowered by the Holy Spirit so that we can live out a life guided by love.

We must go through much soul searching concerning our whole way of living and understanding, for we are called to risk all in order to faithfully trust and follow a supernatural God. Where are we to turn for help in our soul searching? Thankfully, God shows us the reality of Jesus when we participate in a faith community that encourages us to receive the Holy Spirit and be kindled with the fire of divine love that entices us to pursue God's will in all things. By entering an abiding relationship with our God and our faith community, we begin to experience something new: a sense of true joy and peace that builds into a hope for something more satisfying and eternal than our current existence. The revelations of God are true gifts that we should embrace and cherish. They guide us from unprofitable and sorrowful labor into a love affair with our God that blossoms into compassion, mercy, and forgiveness toward anyone in need of God's loving touch.

Dear disciple, let us be willing to receive all that God would give us so that we are enabled to withstand any selfish evil or physical trial we encounter. Let us welcome all God offers and experience Holy Spirit power to endure any shame or injustice we may face. Let us be truly faithful to a devout life by abiding in our God and receive ever-increasing hope with each victory over tribulation. The path of Jesus is the only way to know our God more fully; therefore, let us be completely open to receive all that

God would give us. Let us cry out, "Amazing love!" as we become overwhelmed by all the good gifts Jesus delights in giving His faithful followers. Let us live into the reality of God's kingdom by being blessed to be a blessing.

God's Instruction through Community

Do you not know? Have you not heard? The Lord is the everlasting God, the Creator of the ends of the earth. He will not grow tired or weary, and his understanding no one can fathom. He gives strength to the weary and increases the power of the weak. Even youths grow tired and weary, and young men stumble and fall; but those who hope in the Lord will renew their strength. They will soar on wings like eagles; they will run and not grow weary, they will walk and not be faint.

—ISAIAH 40:28–31 (NIV)

As disciples of our Lord Jesus, we should hunger for ways to more closely experience the presence of our God and receive divine truth concerning the ways of living in community. To this end, we are often encouraged to attend Christian retreats for more focused training on the ways of Jesus. The disciple who pursues this path often finds the most amazing and perhaps overwhelming experience of God's love and forgiveness being shared by fellow Christians. The result of such an encounter with the body of Christ can produce a fervent desire for prayer, study, and service in order to honor and glorify God. Clarity as to our true purpose in God's kingdom gives us a new appreciation for the necessity of our faith community. Our community teaches us of the difficulty in living out life as a true follower of Jesus, for the world we briefly retreated from has not changed. We must understand that pursuing God is risky business, for God calls us to abandon our precious, self-made world in order to experience our newfound joy of God's abiding presence. By choosing God over self, we are enabled to understand the woes of human existence and why God calls us to service in the midst of these woes. Without the assurances we receive from God by the practice of spiritual disciplines, we will remain paralyzed in our puny faith. We must take responsibility for our ignorance and declare that we too want to be faithful disciples of Jesus.

Until we truly know our Savior and the power He wields through the faith community, we cannot bear the burden of this corruptible life without becoming weary and discouraged. Without Jesus by our side, we risk losing hope for family and friends, for our nation, and even for our faith community. It is only by the power of God that we are enabled to endure the weariness and heaviness brought on by this mortal life. When we allow Jesus's teachings to lead us into an attitude of humility, we see others and ourselves differently and understand that our outward good works bring refreshment to us and hope to others as we experience God's presence in community.

Dear disciple, let us always remember that God's reality is only felt in the midst of our faith community as we give ourselves in fellowship and in service to those in need. It is in community that we receive the assurances of God's promises. It is in community that we understand the ways of love, joy, peace, faith, mercy, compassion, self-control, trust, and hope. Our faith community supports us and helps us overcome our anxieties and instructs us in learning inward peace for our souls. Our faith community opens wide scripture so that our hearts and minds may be opened as well. Our faith community helps us learn to abide in our God, where we find true meaning and purpose for our lives. Let us commit our lives to fully experiencing the presence of our God by binding ourselves to other faithful followers of Jesus so that we truly become the hands and feet of Christ Jesus to our lost and weary world.

Are We Worthy?

And this was his message: "After me comes the one more powerful than I, the straps of whose sandals I am not worthy to stoop down and untie. I baptize you with water, but he will baptize you with the Holy Spirit."

—MARK 1:7–8 (NIV)

As disciples of our Lord Jesus, we discover many unpleasant truths when we ask God to give us discernment concerning our human condition. We are given new eyes to see and appreciate our God with awe and wonder as we come to grips with what is means to be created in the divine image. This realization may cause us to fall on our knees and like Isaiah cry out that we are unworthy beings with unclean, sinful lips (Isaiah 6:5 NIV). The psalmist would have us gaze at God's creation in wonder and, like king David, ask why God would be mindful of poor, insignificant us (Psalm 8:3–4 NIV). We might decide like John the Baptist that we are unworthy to untie Jesus's sandals (Mark 1:7 NIV). In fact, our journey as disciples may, at times, tempt us to believe that we are not worthy of any consolation from God. We may even go so far as to think we are only deserving of chastisement and punishment because of our grievously sinful lives. Let's face it: scripture tells us that we have no meritorious works that qualify us for anything from God. Are we not guilty of sin and slow to repent and make amends toward those we have offended? Are we sincere in our confessions, or are we guilty of lip service to our God? Are we willing to face the truth that we are stiff-necked and resist God's call to a better life found in the abiding presence of the Holy Spirit? Even though the revelations of God present very ugly truths to us, we must never forget the greater reality of how much our God loves us in spite of who we are.

The revelation of God's love for His creation through our Savior, Jesus, shows us that we can know and affirm much about the grace of our God. We should be amazed by God's compassion and mercy, which rescue us from perishing in our sin. We should be in awe that through God's long-suffering and patience, we are given chance after chance to understand God's love and forgiveness and experience God's joy and peace. We should be overwhelmed when God stands as our redeemer and mediator despite our guilt, all because we put our trust in our Savior, Jesus. Even though we are deserving of scorn and contempt, we have hope because of God's gracious, loving, and merciful gift that rescues us from despair. We cry out, "Lord Jesus Christ, Son of the living God, have mercy on me, a sinner!" Instead of receiving the death penalty, we receive the intimate embrace of forgiveness and a holy kiss of love from our Creator.

Dear disciple, let us face the truth of who we are before our God and admit our guilt, and then let us receive God's loving touch of forgiveness that washes away the guilt of our sin. Let us approach our God with confidence, knowing that when we confess our sins with humble and contrite hearts, we will be greeted with forgiveness and reconciliation. Let us boldly embrace our God and be bathed in the healing balm of the Holy Spirit. Let us allow God's living water to be our source of cleansing that washes away all defilement. Let us allow our whole being to be enveloped by the presence of the Holy Spirit and know intimately the ways of Jesus. Let us become divine image bearers for God's glory and be empowered to reflect Jesus to everyone we meet.

The Grace of God

But because of his great love for us, God, who is rich in mercy, made us alive with Christ even when we were dead in transgressions—it is by grace you have been saved. And God raised us up with Christ and seated us with him in the heavenly realms in Christ Jesus, in order that in the coming ages he might show the incomparable riches of his grace, expressed in his kindness to us in Christ Jesus. For it is by grace you have been saved, through faith—and this is not from yourselves, it is the gift of God—not by works, so that no one can boast. For we are God's handiwork, created in Christ Jesus to do good works, which God prepared in advance for us to do.

—EPHESIANS 2:4–10 (NIV)

As disciples of our Lord Jesus, we often encounter the term "the grace of God," but how should we understand it? In Hebrew scripture, we see grace as God's faithful love and divine favor given to those who choose to live a holy and pleasing life dedicated to obeying God's commandments. Jesus clarifies the life pleasing to God by summarizing the holy commandments as loving our God and our neighbor with our whole being. Loving in this way is clearly demonstrated by the life and teachings of Jesus and by His faithful followers who have chosen to embrace the grace of God. It is so important for us to understand that the gift of grace is given freely to those who believe, trust, and follow Jesus, who is the way, truth, and life we so desperately need. The grace of God is not and cannot be earned by us, for nothing we do qualifies us to receive this gift. The grace of God is freely given to anyone who is willing to believe and receive the truths of God.

So what makes this gift so attractive that we should desire it above all else? There are many who do not see the advantages because the gift was presented poorly. Others may not listen because they believe the gift too costly to pursue. But we who have chosen to receive God's grace have been divinely touched in a way that opens a new world of understanding and reality. We hear God's Word speak of new life that brings excitement and challenge to our lives previously devoid of meaning and purpose.

Our new grace-infused lives cause us to look in awe at all creation as we wonder why anyone would refuse God's precious gift. This new life invites us to gather as a faith community and share in the challenges of faithfully following the ways of Jesus. We begin to see the obstacles to receiving God's grace and identify them as worldly pleasures and occupations that pollute our minds with temporal consolations. We study the writings of scripture as well as that of saints, old and new, who advocate spiritual practices to overcome our selfish views and actions. We are instructed to balance our time between things done alone and things done in community in order to live fully into the providential plan of God. Our prideful self will tempt us to go it alone, but Jesus reminds us of the importance of community by saying that "where two or three are gathered, I am with you" (Matthew 18:20 NIV).

Dear disciple, please know that time spent alone with God in prayer and scripture reading is precious and should be cherished, but to encounter God fully and understand His ways more clearly, we must come together in worship and study as community. It is in community that we experience the power of God and understand the true meaning of grace, all because of the meritorious and sacrificial life of Christ Jesus, our Lord and Savior. It is in community that we experience love, compassion, mercy, and forgiveness in a tangible way. It is here that the grace of God becomes real and helpful in our time of need. Let us, therefore, throw off our prideful, selfish ways and fully embrace the grace of God. This is our only way to experience true life, joy, and peace.

God's Rescue

So I find this law at work: Although I want to do good, evil is right there with me. For in my inner being I delight in God's law; but I see another law at work in me, waging war against the law of my mind and making me a prisoner of the law of sin at work within me. What a wretched man I am! Who will rescue me from this body that is subject to death? Thanks be to God, who delivers me through Jesus Christ our Lord! So then, I myself in my mind am a slave to God's law, but in my sinful nature a slave to the law of sin.

—ROMANS 7:21–25 (NIV)

As disciples of our Lord Jesus, it is sometimes hard for us to understand or adequately describe why we struggle in doing that which is pleasing to God. Thank goodness God has inspired saints with words that greatly help us in our understanding. Scripture is rich with the cries of God's faithful seeking help in their times of need. The words "rescue me" are heard hundreds of times throughout the Bible from those knowing they have insufficient resources and power to remain faithful to their God. As to our own struggles to remain faithful, the apostle Paul gives us great insight in his letter to the Romans. He describes a war within us between what we naturally know and desire and the blessed life God reveals as the most excellent way. We who have chosen to follow Jesus must agree with Paul that our actions often fail to reflect the godly truth revealed to our minds. As masters of excuses, we must first admit our helplessness if we are to move forward. We hear that we must be "born from above," that we must have "renewed minds," and that we must have "circumcised hearts" before our lives begin to reflect the ways of Jesus on a consistent basis. Scripture uses the "heart" metaphor to describe our "natural" self, which is bound up in our selfish desires and motives. Our natural self has a powerful hold on us and resists our godly inspired desires to repent, that is, to change our ways to love as Jesus loves and to live for God's glory in community.

It is important to recognize and understand our enemy in order to appreciate the necessity of receiving the grace required to transform our minds and overcome our natural selves. Our enemy is crafty, bent on ensnaring and deceiving us in an attempt to sway us to satisfy only self. Our earthly self is stubborn, not willing to be subdued or made subject to any authority. It is lazy and demanding, feeling entitled and lashing out when challenged. It is covetous and stingy, only wanting to receive rather than give. It is proud and boisterous, wanting to be the center of attention and shunning humility. It is arrogant, quick to complain, and enthralled with gossip. There is ugliness behind its disguise, and it avoids God's revealing light at all costs.

Dear disciple, we must let the supernatural light of God's grace permeate us through and through every moment of every day if we are to have any chance of victory over self. We must know our enemy well and cry, "Rescue me!" if we are to ever bear the image of Jesus to a lost world. Let us, therefore, invite daily visitations from God and regularly seek the fellowship of our faith community so that we are empowered to become more than conquerors for God's kingdom and are freed from self to love as we should (Romans 8:37–39 NIV).

Coruling with God

So God created human beings in his own image. In the image of God he created them; male and female he created them. Then God blessed them and said, "Be fruitful and multiply. Fill the earth and govern it. Reign over the fish in the sea, the birds in the sky, and all the animals that scurry along the ground."

—GENESIS 1:27–28 (NLT)

When we study the creation story in scripture, we hear God's Word tell us that we are created in God's image. As disciples of our Lord Jesus, we should appreciate the awesome title and responsibility our Creator has given us. Scripture says that we have been given special rank in creation and the privilege of coruling creation with our God, which should give us pause to consider how we should interact with all created things and beings. Unfortunately, the sinfulness of our human condition causes a breach in our connection with our God, resulting in confusion concerning our privileged responsibilities. This should greatly concern us as scripture points out the consequences for poor ruling. Even though humankind has been created in God's image, there is only one human in all of history to correctly bear the image of God: our Lord Jesus. We may object and say that Jesus was also God, but that does not let us off the hook. From the beginning, God has offered divine grace as our help for success in the tasks of life. Scripture abounds with stories that testify to God's blessed presence in guiding the faithful with loving-kindness, divine favor, and gracious mercy toward the importance of love, forgiveness, and reconciliation. It is up to us to turn to our God and receive the precious grace that God offers so freely.

Are we unwilling to look around and see the consequences of poor image bearing? Are we too stubborn to see the problem of our human condition? Do we cherish our sin so much that we are unwilling to receive God's grace and be empowered for the royal tasks for which we were created? Do we delight in remaining ignorant concerning God's will so we can continue to wallow in our sin rather than reflect the image of Jesus to our broken world? Will we not admit that without God we are but dust and ashes?

Dear disciple, let us pray to God daily to help us truly appreciate the value of divine grace. God's saving grace frees us from our narrow, selfish views and enables our minds to see with godly vision the wonders of creation. God's grace is the treasure of great value and the pearl of great price for which we should give up all else for its gain (Matthew 13:44–46 NIV). God's grace is the power that forms the kingdom of God and binds us to our God and to each other. Let us choose to pursue our royal role, cry out to our God, and receive grace upon grace until we can say that godliness is our greatest desire, that humility will be our mantle, and that love will be our motive in all we say and do.

Bearing Our Cross Revisited

Then he called the crowd to him along with his disciples and said: "Whoever wants to be my disciple must deny themselves and take up their cross and follow me. For whoever wants to save their life will lose it, but whoever loses their life for me and for the gospel will save it. What good is it for someone to gain the whole world, yet forfeit their soul? Or what can anyone give in exchange for their soul?"

—MARK 8:34–37 (NIV)

As disciples of our Lord Jesus, do we understand Jesus's call to, "Take up your cross and follow me" (Mark 8:34 NIV)? After much instruction and study, we usually conclude that this teaching refers to dying to self or, as the apostle Paul puts it, "to be crucified with Christ" (Galatians 2:20 NIV), whereby we no longer live only to satisfy our selfish desires. It is important for us to understand that Jesus expects a rather radical break from our past thinking. The required transformation of our minds allows us to truly appreciate God's truths concerning loving both God and others. Upon receiving this divine instruction, some have chosen very ascetic practices living in isolation from the world and enjoying only the most basic needs. Others have even added bodily punishment in an attempt to bring the sinful flesh under control, but Jesus teaches us that the way of victory lies in perfect surrender of one's will to God and allowing oneself to be born anew, born from above. This miraculous transformation occurs only by receiving the gift of God's grace and by entrusting the Holy Spirit to empower us and intervene for us.

Jesus constantly challenged His disciples and challenges us with godly expectations concerning how we are to live in unity and harmony as community in the kingdom of God. We hear Jesus tell us that we are to be perfect as His Father in heaven is perfect (Matthew 5:48 NIV), which we often misunderstand as an impossible call to sacrifice everything for our salvation. Jesus's disciples became so frustrated and upset that they finally cried out, "Who can be saved?" (Matthew 19:25 NIV). Jesus calmly tells us that we cannot understand or see the way without God's presences in our lives. Jesus bluntly says that we are powerless by our own will and resources to achieve godly perfection. Perfection is possible only with God's help for Jesus says, "All things are possible with God!" (Matthew 19:26 NIV). We must hear this divine truth clearly and apply this teaching to Jesus's command to take up our cross and see that bearing our cross daily is in fact allowing the presence of God to transform us into a new creation capable of doing all God asks of us. In our transformation, we begin to reorder our priorities and trust that God's way is our way to truth, happiness, and satisfaction in all aspects of life. We gradually come to understand what Jesus means in saying, "I am the way and the truth," that leads to the life of our heart's desire (John 14:6 NIV).

Jesus's words "If you love me, keep my commandments" (John 14:15 NKJV) become the transforming message that changes the narrow way of Jesus from a list of burdensome tasks to a path of sweetness and delight.

Dear disciple, let us pray that we see our cross with new understanding in the light of God. Let us ask God to open our eyes to see that our crosses are not burdens but gifts through which God's promises are fulfilled. Let us embrace our crosses while knowing they are the path to paradise where we may behold our King in all His glory. Let us strengthen our faith in our God by praying, "I believe, help me with my unbelief" (Mark 9:24 NKJV).

Do Not Despair in Your Failures

Blessed is the one whose transgressions are forgiven, whose sins are covered. Blessed is the one whose sin the Lord does not count against them and in whose spirit is no deceit. When I kept silent, my bones wasted away through my groaning all day long. For day and night your hand was heavy on me; my strength was sapped as in the heat of summer. Then I acknowledged my sin to you and did not cover up my iniquity. I said, "I will confess my transgressions to the Lord." And you forgave the guilt of my sin.

—PSALM 32:1–5 (NIV)

As disciples of our Lord Jesus, we delight in hearing the good news that our sinful nature has been forgiven and that we are now reconciled to our God; however, the fact that we are not perfect and continue to make poor choices can weigh heavily upon us. The guilt of our sins can often become an obstacle to our progress in following the ways of Jesus. It is a troubling thing to admit that we are repeat offenders with particular sinful acts and wonder if our so-called repentance is merely hypocrisy and an offense to God. Even if we hold to the promise that our sins are forgiven and remember Jesus saying that there is unlimited forgiveness from God as long as we seek repentance with good intentions, we still struggle with the certainty of this confusing truth. God's offer of love and forgiveness despite our sinfulness is not logical to our limited minds. We know that we are guilty of repeated sinful acts and that we have done nothing worthy of forgiveness other than believing the good news of Jesus. When we let our logical minds persuade us that we are not worthy of God's forgiveness, we become subject to a most unhealthy condition that poisons our souls and destroys our relationships with God and others.

It takes much time in earnest prayer with our God and time in sharing with our faith community to overcome this corrupt thinking. We must be convinced of a new reality that says that the supernaturally powered and often illogical kingdom of God has become a reality in our world because of Jesus. Once we begin to trust in this new reality, we become receptive to all the promises Jesus made on behalf of the Father. After all, don't we believe that the Father, Son, and Holy Spirit are one and that their eternal promises are true?

The unpleasant truth is that we have not fully invited God to give us victory over particular sinful acts. In giving God permission to overcome our rationalized addictions, we can experience the reality of the Holy Spirit's presence in our lives, which allows God to recreate us into our intended divine image as one who has been born from above. With profound gratitude, we should accept and receive the multifaceted grace of God and allow divine grace to heal our minds and bodies. We no longer have to constantly beat ourselves up over our failures as disciples. Our new reality instructs us to run to the arms of Jesus found in our faith community, for it is the body of Christ that brings healing to our troubled souls.

Dear disciple, let us grow our faith so that we can quiet any tormenting storms swirling in our minds with the sweet touch of God's grace. Let us abide in our God and our faith community so that we become assured of Jesus's transforming words of hope, forgiveness, and love. Let us not despair in our sinful acts but experience the loving, forgiving touch of our God through true repentance. Let us commit to allowing God to help us overcome all obstacles to perfection so that we achieve sweet victory. Let us meditate on the words of the hymn "Tis So Sweet to Trust in Jesus" until the kingdom of God becomes our reality.

Folly in Scrutinizing the Ways of God

Then some Pharisees and teachers of the law came to Jesus from Jerusalem and asked, "Why do your disciples break the tradition of the elders? They don't wash their hands before they eat!" Jesus replied, "And why do you break the command of God for the sake of your tradition?"

—MATTHEW 15:1–3 (NIV)

Whoever teaches otherwise and does not agree with the sound words of our Lord Jesus Christ and the teaching that is in accordance with godliness, is conceited, understanding nothing, and has a morbid craving for controversy and for disputes about words. From these come envy, dissension, slander, base suspicions, and wrangling among those who are depraved in mind and bereft of the truth, imagining that godliness is a means of gain.

—1 TIMOTHY 6:3–5 (NRSV)

As disciples of our Lord Jesus, we are charged with the task of building up the kingdom of God. We hear the inspired writers of the Hebrew scriptures tell us clearly who our God is and what He expects from us, and to make sure we get it right, God came as Jesus to clear up any confusion. To be sure, the ways of God are sometimes mysterious, but this fact has not stopped many from trying to justify their particular views on these mysteries. It seems that part of our human condition objects to unexplained mysteries, which drives us to formulate rational explanations to ease our minds. Jesus has set for us the standard we should follow as to loving our God and our neighbor in order to build His kingdom, yet our inquisitive minds and arrogant pride lead us into competition over who best understands God's Word and how God's judgments work. Even though scripture says that God's thoughts and ways are not like ours, we say to ourselves, "Isn't that nice?" and then begin to define and categorize every aspect of God we can think of until we reach a dead end. Then we begin to speculate on things that are not entirely clear until our minds come up with theories that sometime turn into doctrines that tear the kingdom of God to pieces. It is true that much of scripture is very clear, but concerning the mysteries of God, we should remember that our God blesses the peacemaker and not the bringer of dissension. We are told over and over that the fear of the Lord is the beginning of wisdom, so should we not stand in awe and wonder of God's mysteries rather than discuss and dissect them? Do we not recognize that God's ways are righteous and just and often beyond our comprehension?

We should listen to Jesus tell us to become like little children if we want to enter the kingdom of heaven. Here we see awe, wonder, trust, and dependence lifted up as traits highly valued in God's kingdom. Do we really want to hear Jesus accuse us of lifting our human interpretations and traditions above God's commandments? Woe to us if we hold our educated guesses concerning the mysteries of God as standards by which we judge others. With this arrogant position, we look down on others in our superiority and feel that it is our duty to correct poor, misguided disciples to a better way (our way) of seeing God. We turn on our fellow Christians and treat them as sons and daughters of perdition rather than brothers and sisters in Christ.

Dear disciple, shall we continue to break God's heart with such behavior? Shall we continue to turn a blind eye to our arrogant pride? Are we willing to admit to how deeply sin run in us? Are we willing to let God the Father, our Lord Jesus, and the Holy Spirit sift us as wheat to remove this impurity? Let us pray continuously for God to reveal our deepest, darkest self and hear Him ask, "Why do you cling to and cherish such ugliness?"

Trusting in God Alone

May the God of hope fill you with all joy and peace as you trust in him, so that you may overflow with hope by the power of the Holy Spirit.

—ROMANS 15:13 (NIV)

As disciples of our Lord Jesus, we are taught to believe that our hope is found in God alone and that we should trust the Holy Spirit for guidance, strength, and provision for all of life's needs. Yet saying that we believe this and living one's life according to this belief are completely different propositions. We must allow God to wake us up to this reality and quit rationalizing our lack of action in building up the kingdom of God. The serious disciple understands the radical changes required in order to possess the mind of Christ that is solely dedicated to fulfilling the will of God. We must be committed to learning how to abide continually in the presence or our Triune God, and this is learned only with the help of our faith community. The result of clinging to our selfish will is to be lost in a hypocritical world that brings shame to our God and our fellow disciples. God's kingdom is designed to work when we are all bound together by the Holy Spirit in unity of purpose. Blindness and corrupt thinking must be removed for us to see this truth; therefore, we must pray continually to God for divine revelation so that we can truly allow God's involvement in the smallest and seemingly most insignificant details of our lives.

We are sometimes tempted to focus on our salvation and the promise of eternal life and see them as future things. What about our present lives? Should we dwell on the future and ignore living in the now? To be true disciples, we must appreciate the great tasks before us. Overcoming self should be seen as the greatest battle of our lives if we are ever to be equipped to give proper glory to our God. We must fall so deeply in love with God that all other priorities are cast aside. We should hear the demands of Jesus as to the requirements to follow Him if we are to take discipleship seriously. Many of the teachings of our Lord Jesus seem harsh until God reveals the truth behind these commands.

We who have persevered can reflect on the troubling and confusing events of our lives and now see how the loving and nurturing hand of God has rescued and redeemed us, validating the truth of Jesus's teachings. We can also look with compassion on those in the midst of these necessary trials who continue to struggle with trusting and hoping in God. Only God can make sense out of life's struggles, so we must cling to God at all costs in order to see the truth.

Dear disciple, let us continue to run with perseverance the good race for God's glory and not give up because of the hardness of life. Let us allow God to purify us so that we become acceptable and holy dwellings for God's divine presence. Let us be possessed by the Holy Spirit and allow Jesus to work through us for the building of God's kingdom here on earth. Let us truly love our God and our neighbor in the now of life and enjoy the blessings of joy and peace both today and forevermore.

Holy Communion

While they were eating, Jesus took bread, and when he had given thanks, he broke it and gave it to his disciples, saying, "Take and eat; this is my body." Then he took a cup, and when he had given thanks, he gave it to them, saying, "Drink from it, all of you. This is my blood of the covenant, which is poured out for many for the forgiveness of sins. I tell you, I will not drink from this fruit of the vine from now on until that day when I drink it new with you in my Father's kingdom."

—MATTHEW 26:26–29 (NIV)

When he was at the table with them, he took bread, gave thanks, broke it and began to give it to them. Then their eyes were opened and they recognized him, and he disappeared from their sight … Then the two told what had happened on the way, and how Jesus was recognized by them when he broke the bread.

—LUKE 24:30–31, 35 (NIV)

As disciples of our Lord Jesus, have we taken the time to plumb the depths concerning the precious sacrament we call Holy Communion? This meal established by Jesus at the Last Supper is designed to emotionally draw us into remembrance concerning all that God has done to reconcile us, and creation, to Himself. This meal that focuses on Jesus's body and blood transforms our understanding of bread and wine into sacred elements used in remembrance of our Lord. We are drawn into the ancient meal of Passover, whereby the Hebrew people remember God's salvation and redemption of their ancestors from Egyptian slavery. We see Jesus as the perfect sacrificial lamb remembered in the Passover meal, whose atoning and efficacious blood replaces the blood of countless animals whose sacrifice resulted only in the temporary forgiveness of sin. We see the pure and sinless body of Jesus in the unleavened bread that was declared "clean and holy" by God at the first Passover free from any impure element unfit for a holy meal. We see yeast represented as the ever-present sin in our lives and remember Jesus condemning the evil, corrupting influences found in the teachings of those who refused to understand the true nature of the kingdom of God.

We first hear this meal called the "Lord's Supper" by the apostle Paul as he describes the order of worship to the Corinthian church in 1 Corinthians 11:17–34. We also hear this meal called the "Eucharist," which is derived from a Greek word denoting "Thanksgiving." We often use the term "Holy Communion" as a rich depiction of what this meal represents. *Holy* says that this meal is set apart specifically for God's purpose, and *Communion* says that we, who are set apart for God, are now a community of faithful followers of Jesus who have gathered in a shared unity as the body of Christ. We share this meal to remember the generous gift of God's love and forgiveness and receive this sacrament as a confirmation of God's presence with us both individually and communally.

What was once guarded and administered by Levitical priests is now available to all because of our Lord Jesus. Jesus's crucifixion, resurrection, and ascension to God the Father have thrown open wide the gracious arms of our God to receive anyone with a repentant heart. Holy Communion has been described as a "means of grace" that we understand as an encounter with our God in a real and tangible way. Bread that was once kept in the temple and eaten only by priests is now available to all. Blood that was once forbidden to eat is now consumed as the life-giving elixir of forgiveness.

Dear disciple, as we approach the altar to receive the body and blood of our Lord, let us hold these thoughts in our minds. Let us remember everything represented in this meal, which transforms us into a new creation. Let us receive these sacred elements as if they are a blessed kiss from our Creator, who reminds us that we are loved, that we are forgiven, and that we are called to be the hands and feet of our Lord Jesus to a needy and broken world.

Printed in the United States
by Baker & Taylor Publisher Services